D0464253

For current pricing information,
or to learn more about this or any Nextext title,
call us toll-free at **1-800-323-5435**
or visit our web site at www.nextext.com.

A HISTORICAL READER

World **War I**

nextext

Cover photograph: *Canadian troops going "over the top" during training near St. Pol, France, October, 1916.* Courtesy Library of Congress.

Printed in the United States of America
ISBN 0-618-00364-9

2 3 4 5 6 7 8 9 0 — QKT — 06 05 04 03 02 01

Table of Contents

Vocabulary words appear in boldface type and are footnoted.
Specialized or technical words and phrases appear in lightface
type and are footnoted.

In the Beginning

CHAPTER 1

A Defining War

THE EDITORIAL PAGE OF THE *WALL STREET JOURNAL*, TUESDAY, NOVEMBER 17, 1998

World War I was a major turning point in the twentieth century. It brought to an end the competition among colonial powers that had characterized the nineteenth century. It ushered in warfare as wholesale slaughter. It destroyed the generation of young European men who gave their lives in its pursuit; they became known as "the lost generation." It laid the groundwork for the rise of communism in Russia. And it left a legacy of bitterness in Germany that proved fertile ground for the rise of Hitler and the Nazis. On the 80th anniversary of the war's end, the following appeared on the editorial page of the Wall Street Journal.

"I led my platoon off to the right and we continued to move steadily across that muddy waste until I realized that we were walking into a curtain of fire . . . [W]e all dived into shell-holes. . . . With my head just over the edge of my shell-hole I lay blinking into the shrieking, crashing hail of death 30 yards in front . . . Dully I hoisted myself out of the mud and gave the signal to advance, which was answered by every man rising and stepping unhesitatingly into the barrage. The effect was so strik-ing that I felt no more that awful dread of shell-fire, but followed them calmly into the crashing, spitting hell until we were surrounded by bursting shells and singing fragments, while above us a stream of bullets added their whining to the general pandemonium. The men were wonderful! And it was astounding that although no one ran or ducked, whilst many were blown over by shells bursting at our very feet, no one was touched until we were through the thickest part of the barrage and making for the little ridge in front. Then I saw fellows drop lifeless while others began to stagger and limp. . . ."

—Edwin Campion Vaughan, "Some Desperate Glory: The World War I Diary of a British Officer"

On an ordinary day, World War I can seem as distant as the Civil War, there being so many more recent horrors competing for our attention. But to commemorate the 80th anniversary of the Armistice[1] in the **penultimate**[2] year of the century is to acknowledge that far from being remote, it is still very much with us. More, possibly, than we know.

The tragedy of war is indivisible. No death or group of deaths is more deserving of our sympathy than any other. Nonetheless, a unique **poignancy**[3] attaches to the memory of World War I. As much as the loss of life, we mourn the loss of innocence, in a generation and a century.

Anxious young men conscripted into World War II, Korea and Vietnam—even those who readied them-selves for the Battles of Trafalgar or Waterloo—could look to previous conflict for some sense of what lay

---

[1] Armistice—the end of World War I, on November 11, 1918.

[2] **penultimate**—next to last.

[3] **poignancy**—state of being profoundly moving or touching.

ahead of them. Not so the class of August 1914. They mustered in[4] believing war was formations, cavalry and bright plumage. Under their feet it turned into mud, the trenches and mechanized mass killing—Vaughan's "curtain of fire."

That curtain divided the old world from the new. More than of World War II, Korea or Vietnam, we are children of the Great War. Almost every aspect of life— our history, our politics, our culture and our outlook— has been enduringly marked by what happened between 1914 and 1918. The First World War famously spawned the second, and much that followed.

The cultural historian Paul Fussell has argued that our **pervasive**[5] attitude of irony was born during World War I, in the bitter recognition of the discrepancy between reality as it was described then—"the war to end all war"—and as it was. Even in our time, the development of precision weaponry such as cruise missiles reflects a sensitivity to the human cost of war, a concept virtually alien to 19th century culture that dates from the engagements like Ypres and the Somme,[6] where casualties could run to 90%.

Some eight million men died during World War I, a shocking figure at the time and one that still gives pause. Even today, plows in France churn up the bones of those consumed in the curtain of fire, their unquiet rest **emblematic**[7] of the century they **midwifed**[8] but didn't live to see.

---

[4] mustered in—entered military service.

[5] **pervasive**—tending to spread or go throughout.

[6] Ypres and the Somme—two particularly bloody battles during World War I.

[7] **emblematic**—symbolic.

[8] **midwifed**—assisted in producing or bringing forth.

QUESTIONS TO CONSIDER

1. In what ways did World War I lead to a "loss of innocence"?

2. According to the article, how did World War I differ from the wars that came before it and those that came after?

3. Do you agree that we are all "children of the Great War"? Explain your opinion.

Men's Nerves Were on Edge

BY A. J. P. TAYLOR

In his book From Sarajevo to Potsdam, *British historian A. J. P. Taylor sets out to explain the mood in Europe that led to war. (The title refers to the Bosnian city of Sarajevo, where Archduke Francis Ferdinand was assassinated in the incident that ignited the war, and Potsdam, the German city where the victorious Allies planned the administration of Germany after the war.) Despite talk of war and the readying of armies, the European great powers, says Taylor, were more at peace than at war in the first part of 1914.*

. . . Peace rested, in fact, on the assumption that, in any dispute, one power or group of powers would give way rather than run the risk of war. Armaments were fondly regarded as a "deterrent," and men said confidently: "If you want peace, prepare for war." Was there some change of spirit in 1914 which made this confidence less justified? Some historians say so. They assert that tension between the Great Powers was mounting and that each conflict was more difficult to settle by compromise. There is a good deal to be said on the other side, and maybe the tensions of 1914 seem greater only because they ended in war. Some of the Great Powers were on rather better terms than they had been a few years before. In particular, the three most advanced powers—France, Germany, and Great Britain—showed signs of drawing together at the expense of the two east European empires, Russia and Austria-Hungary. Both France and Great Britain had agreed to cooperate with Germany over the Baghdad railway. Great Britain and Germany contemplated a partition of the Portuguese colonies. Some highly placed Germans wanted to **jettison**[1] their alliance with Austria-Hungary, while French politicians of the Left were equally cool towards Russia.

Perhaps war was becoming more likely in a vaguer, emotional way. Violence was penetrating political life. Rebellion threatened in Ulster.[2] Suffragettes[3] practiced direct action throughout Great Britain. Industrial disputes provoked armed conflict in Russia and Italy. The Austrian parliament had been suspended as unmanageable. Most curiously, the traditional standards of art and culture were being broken down, as if artists unconsciously anticipated the destruction of the Great War. A new art gallery in Vienna, named Sezession, symbolized this spirit of revolt. The Futurists[4] were knocking the sense out of poetry. The Cubists[5] were creating abstract, geometrical forms, thus ending a tradition of representational art which had dominated Europe for five

---

[1] **jettison**—to cast overboard or off.

[2] Ulster—former province of Ireland.

[3] Suffragettes—women who fought for the right of women to vote.

[4] Futurists—artists, musicians, or writers who preferred to capture the sensation of movement and growth in objects, rather than their appearance at a particular point in time.

[5] Cubists—artists who embraced Cubism, a style of painting, drawing, and sculpture in which objects are represented by cubes and other geometric forms rather than by realistic details.

hundred years. The Cubist movement drew on nearly all European countries and counted Russians, Poles, Germans, Spaniards among its principal exponents. In music, Schoenberg, Berg, and Webern sounded a discordant note against the **diatonic**[6] scale. In 1913, Stravinsky's *Rite of Spring* provoked days of rioting in Paris. Previously artists had been Bohemians; now they were rebels, proudly displaying their hostility to society. Men's nerves were on edge—or so we surmise in retrospect.

. . . All the Great Powers had elaborate plans for mobilizing their vast armies. Only the Germans merged these into plans for actual war. The others could mobilize and stand still; Germany could not. The German generals and statesmen were prisoners of the railway-timetables which they had worked out in the previous years. Technically the war started because the Germans wanted to get their blow in first. Men had, of course, debated everywhere what their country could gain if war came, and perhaps the Germans had debated a bit more than others. But in August 1914 the aim of the Germans and everyone else was victory for its own sake. The war aims were worked out only after fighting had started.

---

[6] **diatonic**—the eight tones of a standard major or minor scale.

QUESTIONS TO CONSIDER

1. What, in the author's opinion, were the Great Powers fighting for in World War I?

2. What were some of the social, political, and cultural changes that took place in the years immediately prior to World War I?

3. Do you agree with the opinion "If you want peace, prepare for war"? Explain your viewpoint.

August 1, 1914: Berlin

BY BARBARA TUCHMAN

After a nationalist Serb assassin shot the visiting Austrian Archduke Francis Ferdinand, Austria insisted that Serbia submit to a military expedition to put down Austria's enemies within Serbia. Serbia refused. Russia, historically an ally of Serbia, said that if Austria moved against Serbia, then Russia would wage war against Austria. Britain suggested that the problem be settled by a conference of Great Britain, France, Germany, and Italy; but Germany rejected that idea. Austria declared war on Serbia. Russia began to mobilize against Austria, and Germany sent an ultimatum to Russia insisting that Russia immediately pull back its troops and stop mobilizing.

In her famous book The Guns of August *historian Barbara Tuchman details the beginning of the First World War. Here is her account of what happened next. A. J. P. Taylor has said that the Germans were prisoners of the railway timetables they had worked out. Here Tuchman lets us see just how true that was.*

At noon on Saturday, August 1, the German **ultimatum**[1] to Russia expired without a Russian reply. Within an hour a telegram went out to the German ambassador in St. Petersburg instructing him to declare war by five o'clock that afternoon. At five o'clock the Kaiser decreed general mobilization, some preliminaries having already got off to a head start under the declaration of *Kriegesgefahr* (Danger of War) the day before. At five-thirty Chancellor Bethmann-Hollweg, absorbed in a document he was holding in his hand and accompanied by little Jagow, the Foreign Minister, hurried down the steps of the Foreign Office, hailed an ordinary taxi, and sped off to the palace. Shortly afterward General von Moltke, the gloomy Chief of General Staff, was pulled up short as he was driving back to his office with the mobilization order signed by the Kaiser in his pocket. A messenger in another car overtook him with an urgent summons from the palace. He returned to hear a last-minute, desperate proposal from the Kaiser that reduced Moltke to tears and could have changed the history of the twentieth century.

Now that the moment had come, the Kaiser suffered at the necessary risk to East Prussia, in spite of the six weeks' leeway his Staff promised before the Russians could fully mobilize. "I hate the Slavs," he confessed to an Austrian officer. "I know it is a sin to do so. We ought not to hate anyone. But I can't help hating them." He had taken comfort, however, in the news, reminiscent of 1905, of strikes and riots in St. Petersburg, of mobs smashing windows, and "violent street fights between revolutionaries and police." Count Pourtalès, his aged ambassador, who had been seven years in Russia, concluded, and repeatedly assured his government, that Russia would not fight for fear of revolution. Captain von Eggeling, the German military attaché, kept

---

[1] **ultimatum**—a final statement of terms made by one party to another.

repeating the credo about 1916, and when Russia nevertheless mobilized, he reported she planned "no **tenacious**[2] offensive but a slow retreat as in 1812." In the **affinity**[3] for error of German diplomats, these judgments established a record. They gave heart to the Kaiser, who as late as July 31 composed a missive for the "guidance" of his Staff, rejoicing in the "mood of a sick Tom-cat" that, on the evidence of his envoys, he said prevailed in the Russian court and army.

In Berlin on August 1, the crowds milling in the streets and massed in thousands in front of the palace were tense and heavy with anxiety. Socialism, which most of Berlin's workers professed, did not run so deep as their instinctive fear and hatred of the Slavic hordes. Although they had been told by the Kaiser, in his speech from the balcony announcing *Kriegesgefahr* the evening before, that the "sword has been forced into our hand," they still waited in the ultimate dim hope of a Russian reply. The hour of the ultimatum passed. A journalist in the crowd felt the air "electric with rumor. People told each other Russia had asked for an extension of time. The Bourse writhed in panic. The afternoon passed in almost insufferable anxiety." Bethmann-Hollweg issued a statement ending, "If the iron dice roll, may God help us." At five o'clock a policeman appeared at the palace gate and announced mobilization to the crowd, which obediently struck up the national hymn, "Now thank we all our God." Cars raced down Unter den Linden with officers standing up in them, waving handkerchiefs and shouting, "Mobilization!" Instantly converted from Marx to Mars, people cheered wildly and rushed off to vent their feelings on suspected Russian spies, several of whom were pummeled or trampled to death in the course of the next few days.

---

[2] **tenacious**—strong, tending to hold fast.
[3] **affinity**—a natural attraction or feeling of kinship.

Once the mobilization button was pushed, the whole vast machinery for calling up, equipping, and transporting two million men began turning automatically. Reservists went to their designated depots, were issued uniforms, equipment, and arms, formed into companies and companies into battalions, were joined by cavalry, cyclists, artillery, medical units, cook wagons, blacksmith wagons, even postal wagons, moved according to prepared railway timetables to concentration points near the frontier where they would be formed into divisions, divisions into corps, and corps into armies ready to advance and fight. One army corps alone—out of the total of 40 in the German forces—required 170 railway cars for officers, 965 for infantry, 2,960 for cavalry, 1,915 for artillery and supply wagons, 6,010 in all, grouped in 140 trains and an equal number again for their supplies. From the moment the order was given, everything was to move at fixed times according to a schedule precise down to the number of train axles that would pass over a given bridge within a given time.

Confident in his magnificent system, Deputy Chief of Staff General Waldersee had not even returned to Berlin at the beginning of the crisis but had written to Jagow: "I shall remain here ready to jump; we are all prepared at the General Staff; in the meantime there is nothing for us to do." It was a proud tradition inherited from the elder, or "great" Moltke who on mobilization day in 1870 was found lying on a sofa reading *Lady Audley's Secret*.

His enviable calm was not present today in the palace. Face to face no longer with the specter but the reality of a two-front war, the Kaiser was as close to the "sick Tom-cat" mood as he thought the Russians were. More **cosmopolitan**[4] and more timid than the **archetype**[5] Prussian, he had never actually wanted a

---

[4] **cosmopolitan**—worldly; sophisticated.

[5] **archetype**—an original model; a perfect example.

general war. He wanted greater power, greater prestige, above all more authority in the world's affairs for Germany but he preferred to obtain them by frightening rather than by fighting other nations. He wanted the **gladiator's**[6] rewards without the battle, and whenever the prospect of battle came too close, as at Algeciras and Agadir, he shrank.

As the final crisis boiled, his marginalia on telegrams grew more and more agitated: "Aha! the common cheat," "Rot!" "He lies!" "Mr. Grey is a false dog," "Twaddle!" "The rascal is crazy or an idiot!" When Russia mobilized he burst into a **tirade**[7] of passionate foreboding, not against the Slav traitors but against the unforgettable figure of the wicked uncle: "The world will be engulfed in the most terrible of wars, the ultimate aim of which is the ruin of Germany. England, France and Russia have conspired for our annihilation . . . that is the naked truth of the situation which was slowly but surely created by Edward VII. . . . The encirclement of Germany is at last an accomplished fact. We have run our heads into the noose. . . . The dead Edward is stronger than the living I!"

Conscious of the shadow of the dead Edward, the Kaiser would have welcomed any way out of the commitment to fight both Russia and France and, behind France, the looming figure of still-undeclared England.

At the last moment one was offered. A colleague of Bethmann's came to beg him to do anything he could to save Germany from a two-front war and suggested a means. For years a possible solution for Alsace had been discussed in terms of autonomy as a Federal State within the German Empire. If offered and accepted by the Alsatians, this solution would have deprived France of

---

[6] **gladiator's**—those of a fighter in the ancient Roman arena.

[7] **tirade**—a long, angry speech. This one is against his uncle, England's King Edward VII.

any reason to liberate the lost provinces. As recently as July 16, the French Socialist Congress had gone on record in favor of it. But the German military had always insisted that the provinces must remain **garrisoned**[8] and their political rights **subordinated**[9] to "military necessity." Until 1911 no constitution had ever been granted and autonomy never. Bethmann's colleague now urged him to make an immediate, public, and official offer for a conference on autonomy for Alsace. This could be allowed to drag on without result, while its moral effect would force France to refrain from attack while at least considering the offer. Time would be gained for Germany to turn her forces against Russia while remaining stationary in the West, thus keeping England out.

The author of this proposal remains anonymous, and it may be **apocryphal.**[10] It does not matter. The opportunity was there, and the Chancellor could have thought of it for himself. But to seize it required boldness, and Bethmann, behind his distinguished façade of great height, somber eyes, and well-trimmed imperial, was a man, as Theodore Roosevelt said of Taft, "who means well feebly." Instead of offering France an inducement to stay neutral, the German government sent her an ultimatum at the same time as the ultimatum to Russia. They asked France to reply within eighteen hours whether she would stay neutral in a Russo-German war, and added that if she did Germany would "demand as guarantee of neutrality the handing over to us of the fortresses of Toul and Verdun which we shall occupy and restore after the war is over"—in other words, the handing over of the key to the French door.

Baron von Schoen, German ambassador in Paris, could not bring himself to pass on this "brutal" demand

---

[8] **garrisoned**—stationed at a military post.

[9] **subordinated**—made secondary.

[10] **apocryphal**—erroneous or fictitious.

at a moment when, it seemed to him, French neutrality would have been such a supreme advantage to Germany that his government might well have offered to pay a price for it rather than exact a penalty. He presented the request for a statement of neutrality without the demand for the fortresses, but the French, who had intercepted and decoded his instructions, knew of it anyway. When Schoen, at 11:00 A.M. on August 1, asked for France's reply he was answered that France "would act in accordance with her interests."

In Berlin just after five o'clock a telephone rang in the Foreign Office. Under-Secretary Zimmermann, who answered it, turned to the editor of the *Berliner Tageblatt* sitting by his desk and said, "Moltke wants to know whether things can start." At that moment a telegram from London, just decoded, broke in upon the planned proceedings. It offered hope that if the movement against France could be instantly stopped Germany might safely fight a one-front war after all. Carrying it with them, Bethmann and Jagow dashed off on their taxi trip to the palace.

The telegram, from Prince Lichnowsky, ambassador in London, reported an English offer, as Lichnowsky understood it, "that in case we did not attack France, England would remain neutral and would guarantee France's neutrality."

The ambassador belonged to that class of Germans who spoke English and copied English manners, sports, and dress, in a strenuous endeavor to become the very pattern of an English gentleman. His fellow noblemen, the Prince of Pless, Prince Blücher, and Prince Münster were all married to English wives. At a dinner in Berlin in 1911, in honor of a British general, the guest of honor was astonished to find that all forty German guests, including Bethmann-Hollweg and Admiral Tirpitz, spoke English fluently. Lichnowsky differed from his class in that he was not only in manner but in heart an earnest **Anglophile**.[11] He had come to London determined to make himself and his country liked. English society had been lavish with country weekends. To the ambassador no tragedy could be greater than war between the country of his birth and the country of his heart, and he was grasping at any handle to avert it.

When the Foreign Secretary, Sir Edward Grey, telephoned him that morning, in the interval of a Cabinet meeting, Lichnowsky, out of his own anxiety, interpreted what Grey said to him as an offer by England to stay neutral and to keep France neutral in a Russo-German war, if, in return, Germany would promise not to attack France.

Actually, Grey had not said quite that. What, in his **elliptical**[12] way, he offered was a promise to keep France neutral if Germany would promise to stay neutral as against France *and* Russia, in other words, not go to war against either, pending the result of efforts to settle the Serbian affair. After eight years as Foreign Secretary in a period of chronic "Bosnias,"[13] as Bülow called them, Grey had perfected a manner of speaking designed to convey as little meaning as possible; his avoidance of the point-blank, said a colleague, almost amounted to method. Over the telephone, Lichnowsky, himself dazed by the coming tragedy, would have had no difficulty misunderstanding him.

The Kaiser clutched at Lichnowsky's passport to a one-front war. Minutes counted. Already mobilization was rolling **inexorably**[14] toward the French frontier. The first hostile act, seizure of a railway junction in Luxembourg, whose neutrality the five Great Powers, including Germany, had guaranteed, was scheduled within an hour. It must be stopped, stopped at once. But

---

[11] **Anglophile**—one who admires England.

[12] **elliptical**—deliberately obscure or confusing.

[13] chronic "Bosnias"—areas that continually threaten political stability.

[14] **inexorably**—relentlessly; inflexibly.

how? Where was Moltke? Moltke had left the palace. An aide was sent off, with siren screaming, to intercept him. He was brought back.

The Kaiser was himself again, the All-Highest, the War Lord, blazing with a new idea, planning, proposing, disposing. He read Moltke the telegram and said in triumph: "Now we can go to war against Russia only. We simply march the whole of our Army to the East!"

Aghast at the thought of his marvelous machinery of mobilization wrenched into reverse, Moltke refused point-blank. For the past ten years, first as assistant to Schlieffen, then as his successor, Moltke's job had been planning for this day, The Day, *Der Tag,* for which all Germany's energies were gathered, on which the march to final mastery of Europe would begin. It weighed upon him with an oppressive, almost unbearable responsibility.

Tall, heavy, bald, and sixty-six years old, Moltke habitually wore an expression of profound distress which led the Kaiser to call him *der traurige Julius* (or what might be rendered "Gloomy Gus"; in fact, his name was Helmuth). Poor health, for which he took an annual cure at Carlsbad, and the shadow of a great uncle were perhaps cause for gloom. From his window in the red brick General Staff building on the Königplatz where he lived as well as worked, he looked out every day on the equestrian statue of his namesake, the hero of 1870 and, together with Bismarck, the architect of the German Empire. The nephew was a poor horseman with a habit of falling off on staff rides and, worse, a follower of Christian Science with a side interest in anthroposophism[15] and other cults. For this unbecoming weakness in a Prussian officer he was considered "soft"; what is more, he painted, played the cello,

---

[15] anthroposophism—belief that knowledge of the spiritual world could be achieved through a prescribed method of self-discipline.

carried Goethe's *Faust* in his pocket, and had begun a translation of Maeterlinck's *Pelléas et Mélisande.*

Introspective and a doubter by nature, he had said to the Kaiser upon his appointment in 1906: "I do not know how I shall get on in the event of a campaign. I am very critical of myself." Yet he was neither personally nor politically timid. In 1911, disgusted by Germany's retreat in the Agadir crisis, he wrote to Conrad von Hotzendorff that if things got worse he would resign, propose to disband the army and "place ourselves under the protection of Japan; then we can make money undisturbed and turn into imbeciles." He did not hesitate to talk back to the Kaiser, but told him "quite brutally" in 1900 that his Peking expedition was a "crazy adventure," and when offered the appointment as Chief of Staff, asked the Kaiser if he expected "to win the big prize twice in the same lottery"—a thought that had certainly influenced William's choice. He refused to take the post unless the Kaiser stopped his habit of winning all the war games which was making nonsense of maneuvers. Surprisingly, the Kaiser meekly obeyed.

Now, on the climactic night of August 1, Moltke was in no mood for any more of the Kaiser's meddling with serious military matters, or with meddling of any kind with the fixed arrangements. To turn around the deployment of a million men from west to east at the very moment of departure would have taken a more iron nerve than Moltke disposed of. He saw a vision of the deployment crumbling apart in confusion, supplies here, soldiers there, ammunition lost in the middle, companies without officers, divisions without staffs, and those 11,000 trains, each exquisitely scheduled to click over specified tracks at specified intervals of ten minutes, tangled in a grotesque ruin of the most perfectly planned military movement in history.

"Your Majesty," Moltke said to him now, "it cannot be done. The deployment of millions cannot be improvised. If Your Majesty insists on leading the whole army to the East it will not be an army ready for battle but a disorganized mob of armed men with no arrangements for supply. Those arrangements took a whole year of intricate labor to complete"—and Moltke closed upon that rigid phrase, the basis for every major German mistake, the phrase that launched the invasion of Belgium and the submarine war against the United States, the inevitable phrase when military plans dictate policy—"and once settled, it cannot be altered."

In fact it could have been altered. The German General Staff, though committed since 1905 to a plan of attack upon France first, had in their files, revised each year until 1913, an alternative plan against Russia with all the trains running eastward.

"Build no more fortresses, build railways," ordered the elder Moltke who had laid out his strategy on a railway map and **bequeathed**[16] the dogma that railways are the key to war. In Germany the railway system was under military control with a staff officer assigned to every line; no track could be laid or changed without permission of the General Staff. Annual mobilization war games kept railway officials in constant practice and tested their ability to improvise and divert traffic by telegrams reporting lines cut and bridges destroyed. The best brains produced by the War College, it was said, went into the railway section and ended up in lunatic asylums.

When Moltke's "It cannot be done" was revealed after the war in his memoirs, General von Staab, Chief of the Railway Division, was so incensed by what he considered a reproach upon his bureau that he wrote a book to prove it could have been done. In pages of charts and graphs he demonstrated how, given notice on August 1, he could have deployed four out of the

---

[16] **bequeathed**—handed down.

seven armies to the Eastern Front by August 15, leaving three to defend the West. Matthias Erzberger, the Reichstag deputy and leader of the Catholic Centrist Party, has left another testimony. He says that Moltke himself, within six months of the event, admitted to him that the assault on France at the beginning was a mistake and instead, "the larger part of our army ought first to have been sent East to smash the Russian steam roller, limiting operations in the West to beating off the enemy's attack on our frontier."

On the night of August 1, Moltke, clinging to the fixed plan, lacked the necessary nerve. "Your uncle would have given me a different answer," the Kaiser said to him bitterly. The reproach "wounded me deeply" Moltke wrote afterward; "I never pretended to be the equal of the old Field Marshal." Nevertheless he continued to refuse. "My protest that it would be impossible to maintain peace between France and Germany while both countries were mobilized made no impression. Everybody got more and more excited and I was alone in my opinion."

Finally, when Moltke convinced the Kaiser that the mobilization plan could not be changed, the group which included Bethmann and Jagow drafted a telegram to England regretting that Germany's advance movements toward the French border "can no longer be altered," but offering a guarantee not to cross the border before August 3 at 7:00 P.M., which cost them nothing as no crossing was scheduled before that time. Jagow rushed off a telegram to his ambassador in Paris, where mobilization had already been decreed at four o'clock, instructing him helpfully to "please keep France quiet for the time being." The Kaiser added a personal telegram to King George, telling him that for "technical reasons" mobilization could not be **countermanded**[17] at

---

[17] **countermanded**—took back or revoked a command.

this late hour, but "If France offers me neutrality which must be guaranteed by the British fleet and army, I shall of course refrain from attacking France and employ my troops elsewhere. I hope France will not become nervous."

It was now minutes before seven o'clock, the hour when the 16th Division was scheduled to move into Luxembourg. Bethmann excitedly insisted that Luxembourg must not be entered under any circumstances while waiting for the British answer. Instantly the Kaiser, without asking Moltke, ordered his aide-de-camp to telephone and telegraph 16th Division Headquarters at Trier to cancel the movement. Moltke saw ruin again. Luxembourg's railways were essential for the offensive through Belgium against France. "At that moment," his memoirs say, "I thought my heart would break."

Despite all his pleading, the Kaiser refused to budge. Instead, he added a closing sentence to his telegram to King George, "The troops on my frontier are in the act of being stopped by telephone and telegraph from crossing into France," a slight if vital twist of the truth, for the Kaiser could not acknowledge to England that what he had intended and what was being stopped was the violation of a neutral country. It would have implied his intention also to violate Belgium, which would have been *casus belli*[18] in England, and England's mind was not yet made up.

"Crushed," Moltke says of himself, on what should have been the culminating day of his career, he returned to the General Staff and "burst into bitter tears of **abject**[19] despair." When his aide brought him for his signature the written order canceling the Luxembourg movement, "I threw my pen down on the table and

---

[18] *casus belli*—reason for war.

[19] **abject**—of the most miserable kind; wretched.

refused to sign." To have signed as the first order after mobilization one that would have annulled all the careful preparations would have been taken, he knew, as evidence of "hesitancy and irresolution." "Do what you want with this telegram," he said to his aide; "I will not sign it."

He was still brooding at eleven o'clock when another summons came from the palace. Moltke found the Kaiser in his bedroom, characteristically dressed for the occasion, with a military overcoat over his nightshirt. A telegram had come from Lichnowsky, who, in a further talk with Grey, had discovered his error and now wired sadly, "A positive proposal by England is, on the whole, not in prospect."

"Now you can do what you like," said the Kaiser, and went back to bed. Moltke, the Commander in Chief who had now to direct a campaign that would decide the fate of Germany, was left permanently shaken. "That was my first experience of the war," he wrote afterward. "I never recovered from the shock of this incident. Something in me broke and I was never the same thereafter."

QUESTIONS TO CONSIDER

1. Why do you think Commander-in-Chief Moltke is so anxious to see Germany go to war?

2. What do you think would be some of the advantages of fighting a "one-front" war?

3. In what way were the Germans "prisoners of the railway timetables they had worked out"?

from

All Quiet on the Western Front

BY ERICH MARIA REMARQUE

World War I was known afterward as the Great War. The expectation throughout Europe had been that it would be glorious, triumphant (for every side believed it would win), and over quickly. It was none of these things. People said they had "lost their innocence." The poets and novelists who wrote about it described the bitterness and disillusionment felt by all who lived through the Great War. All Quiet on the Western Front *is the most famous novel to come out of the war. This excerpt from the book describes the training that a German soldier received to change him from a privileged, upper-middle-class student into a tough, vicious soldier.*

Once it was different. When we went to the District Commandant to enlist, we were a class of twenty young men, many of whom proudly shaved for the first time before going to the barracks. We had no definite plans for our future. Our thoughts of a career and occupation were as yet of too unpractical a character to furnish any scheme of life. We were still crammed full of vague ideas which gave to life, and to the war also, an ideal and almost romantic character. We were trained in the army for ten weeks and in this time more profoundly influenced than by ten years at school. We learned that a bright button is weightier than four volumes of Schopenhauer.[1] At first astonished, then embittered, and finally indifferent, we recognized that what matters is not the mind but the boot brush, not intelligence but the system, not freedom but drill. We became soldiers with eagerness and enthusiasm, but they have done everything to knock that out of us. After three weeks it was no longer incomprehensible to us that a braided postman should have more authority over us than had formerly our parents, our teachers, and the whole gamut of culture from Plato to Goethe. With our young, awakened eyes we saw that the classical conception of the Fatherland held by our teachers resolved itself here into a **renunciation**[2] of personality such as one would not ask of the meanest servant—salutes, springing to attention, parade-marches, presenting arms, right wheel, left wheel, clicking the heels, insults, and a thousand **pettifogging**[3] details. We had fancied our task would be different, only to find we were to be trained for heroism as though we were circus-ponies. But we soon accustomed ourselves to it. We learned in fact that some part of these things was necessary, but the rest merely show. Soldiers have a fine nose for such distinctions.

By threes and fours our class was scattered over the platoons amongst Frisian fishermen, peasants, and laborers with whom we soon made friends. Kropp,

---

[1] Schopenhauer—German philosopher (1788–1860).

[2] **renunciation**—the act of giving up or rejecting.

[3] **pettifogging**—bickering or quarreling.

Müller, Kemmerich, and I went to No. 9 platoon under Corporal Himmelstoss.

He had the reputation of being the strictest disciplinarian in the camp, and was proud of it. He was a small undersized fellow with a **foxy**,[4] waxed moustache, who had seen twelve years' service and was in civil life a postman. He had a special dislike for Kropp, Tjaden, Westhus, and me, because he sensed a quiet defiance.

I have remade his bed fourteen times in one morning. Each time he had some fault to find and pulled it to pieces. I have kneaded a pair of prehistoric boots that were as hard as iron for twenty hours—with intervals of course—until they became as soft as butter and not even Himmelstoss could find anything more to do to them; under his orders I have scrubbed out the Corporals' Mess with a tooth-brush. Kropp and I were given the job of clearing the barrack-square of snow with a hand-broom and a dust-pan, and we would have gone on till we were frozen had not a lieutenant accidentally appeared who sent us off, and hauled Himmelstoss over the coals. But the only result of this was to make Himmelstoss hate us more. For six weeks consecutively I did guard every Sunday and was hut-orderly for the same length of time. With full pack and rifle I have had to practice on a soft, wet, newly ploughed field the "Prepare to advance, advance!" and the "Lie down!" until I was one lump of mud and finally collapsed. Four hours later I had to report to Himmelstoss with my clothes scrubbed clean, my hands chafed and bleeding. Together with Kropp, Westhus, and Tjaden I have stood at attention in a hard frost without gloves for a quarter of an hour at a stretch, while Himmelstoss watched for the slightest movement of our bare fingers on the steel barrel of the rifle. I have run eight times from the top floor of the barracks down to the courtyard in my shirt

---

[4] **foxy**—reddish-brown.

at two o'clock in the morning because my drawers projected three inches beyond the edge of the stool on which one had to stack all one's things. Alongside me ran the corporal, Himmelstoss, and trod on my bare toes. At bayonet-practice I had constantly to fight with Himmelstoss, I with a heavy iron weapon whilst he had a handy wooden one with which he easily struck my arms till they were black and blue. Once, indeed, I became so infuriated that I ran at him blindly and gave him a mighty jab in the stomach and knocked him down. When he reported me the company commander laughed at him and told him he ought to keep his eyes open; he understood Himmelstoss, and apparently was not displeased at his **discomfiture.**[5] I became a past master on the horizontal bars and strove to surpass my instructor at physical jerks;—we have trembled at the mere sound of his voice, but this runaway post-horse never got the better of us.

One Sunday as Kropp and I were lugging a latrine-bucket on a pole across the barrack-yard, Himmelstoss came by, all polished up and spry for going out. He planted himself in front of us and asked how we liked the job. In spite of ourselves we tripped and emptied the bucket over his legs. He raved, but the limit had been reached.

"That means clink," he yelled.

But Kropp had had enough. "There'll be an inquiry first," he said, "and then we'll unload."

"Mind how you speak to a non-commissioned officer!" bawled Himmelstoss. "Have you lost your senses? You wait till you're spoken to. What will you do, anyway?"

"Show you up, Corporal," said Kropp, his thumbs in line with the seams of his trousers.

---

[5] **discomfiture**—state of embarrassment.

Himmelstoss saw what we meant and went off without saying a word. But before he disappeared he growled: "You'll drink this!"—but it was the end of his authority. He tried it on once more in the ploughed field with his "Prepare to advance, advance" and "Lie down." We obeyed each order, since an order's an order and has to be obeyed. But we did it so slowly that Himmelstoss became desperate. Carefully we went down on our knees, then on our hands, and so on; in the meantime, quite infuriated, he had given another command. But before we had even begun to sweat he was hoarse. After that he left us in peace. He did indeed always refer to us as swine, but there was, nevertheless, a certain respect in his tone.

There were many other staff corporals, the majority of whom were more decent. But above all each of them wanted to keep his good job there at home as long as possible, and that he could do only by being strict with the recruits.

Practically every conceivable polishing job in the entire camp fell to us and we often howled with rage. Many of us became ill through it; Wolf actually died of inflammation of the lung. But we would have felt ridiculous had we hauled down our colors. We became hard, suspicious, pitiless, vicious, tough—and that was good; for these attributes had been entirely lacking in us. Had we gone into the trenches without this period of training most of us would certainly have gone mad. Only thus were we prepared for what awaited us. We did not break down, but endured; our twenty years, which made many another thing so grievous, helped us in this. But by far the most important was that it awakened in us a strong, practical sense of *esprit de corps*,[6] which in the field developed into the finest thing that arose out of the war—comradeship.

[6] *esprit de corps*—strong bond that develops between members of a group.

QUESTIONS TO CONSIDER

1. What causes Himmelstoss's change in attitude toward Kropp and the narrator?

2. What does the narrator see as a benefit of his training?

3. How would you describe the tone of Remarque's writing? Is he angry? bitter? melancholy? Explain with examples.

Europe at War

Map of Europe before World War 1.

Area depicted in maps.

Map of Europe after World War I.

▲

In the Trenches Soldiers on the front line fought from trenches
dug in the ground. Often the trenches filled with water and, later, the
bodies of dead warriors.

Medics prepare to move a wounded soldier to the hospital. ▶

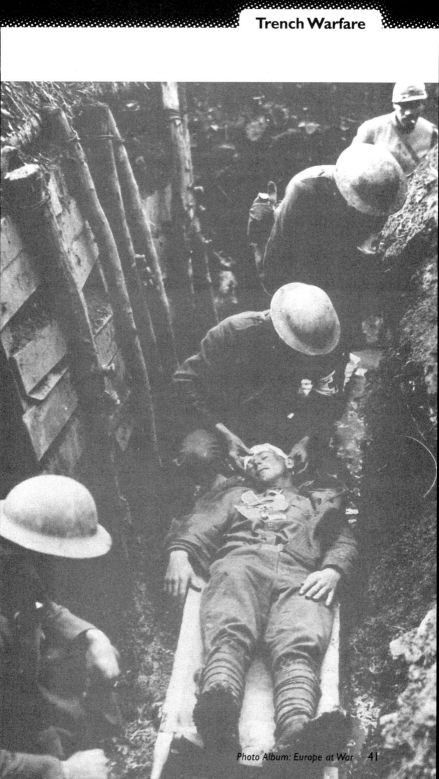

Gaining Ground Wearing pointed metal helmets and bearing rifles with bayonets, the German troops advance against the Allied forces.
▼

▲

Erecting a Barricade Wooden supports baffled by straw make an effective shield against the enemy.

Fighting the War

CHAPTER four

Swords and Spades, Water and Spies

BY LYN MACDONALD

Trench warfare was definitely not the glorious kind of warfare that civilians had expected. Letters and diaries provide a close-up of what it was really like. In this excerpt from her book 1915: The Death of Innocence, Macdonald relies on such sources to paint a graphic picture of warfare on the western front.

It was spades not swords that were wanted in the trenches. And manpower. And muscle-power. And hard grinding labor. The brunt of the work fell on the Royal Engineers.

The 5th Field Company, Royal Engineers, had been out since the beginning. They had dug the Army out of Mons, they had dug trenches for the infantry throughout the long retreat, blown bridges over rivers in full view of the Germans when the last of the infantry had safely crossed, and, when the tide had turned, they built pontoon bridges across the same rivers to take the infantry back, first to the Marne, then to the Aisne, and finally along the long road north as they raced the Germans back to Flanders. The engineers had toiled again at Ypres, digging trenches for reserves and supports and, always under shellfire, throwing up entanglements of barbed wire to protect them. And when the Germans attacked and the troops were pushed back, as the front line gave way, and battalions were **decimated,**[1] the engineers had gone into the trenches and helped the thinning ranks of infantrymen to beat the Germans off. The 5th Field Company had been in at the kill when the last wavering line faltered and briefly gave way, when the Prussian Guard streamed through and every man was needed to try to stop them. In retrospect it had been their moment of glory, for the sappers[2] had flung down their spades, picked up their rifles, formed up with the ragged remnants of the infantry, fixed bayonets and charged into Nonnebosschen Wood to drive the Germans back. It had not seemed very glorious at the time—but it had saved the day.

Now the infantry were returning the favor by turning out working parties night after night to labor alongside the sappers constructing defenses. Working in the flooded marshland to the south of Armentieres where the River Lys, swollen by incessant rain, wound across the water-logged plain and overflowed to mingle with a thousand streams and ditches, even the battle-hardened veterans who had been out since the start of the war agreed that this was the worst yet. It was a waterscape rather than a landscape. Trenches filled up with water as fast as they were dug and the **culverts**[3] and dams they made to divert it merely channeled the flood to another trench in another part of the line. They built bridges across watery trenches that collapsed into the stream with the next

---

[1] **decimated**—destroyed.

[2] sappers—name for men who dug trenches during World War I.

[3] **culverts**—drains.

rainstorm in a cascade of mud as the sodden banks that supported them gave way. They took levels, drew up plans, set up pumps, but still the water rose. The trenches were knee deep in it. The men who manned them, soaking, shivering, plastered from head to foot with mud, reflected bitterly that it was not so much the Germans as the weather that was the **adversary.**[4]

> *Oh, the rain, the mud, and the cold*
> *The cold the mud and the rain.*
> *With weather at zero it's hard for a hero*
> *From language that's rude to refrain.*
> *With porridgy muck to the knees*
> *With the sky that's still pouring a flood,*
> *Sure the worst of our foes*
> *Are the pains and the woes*
> *Of the rain, and the cold and the mud.*
> —Robert Service

Lt. C. Tennant, 1/4 Bn., Seaforth Highlanders (TF), Dehra Dun Brig., Meerut Div.

Water is the great and pressing problem at present, the weather has been almost unprecedently wet and the whole countryside is soaked in mud and like a sponge. Owing to its flatness it is generally impossible to drain the trenches and in many cases those now being held were only taken in the first instance as a temporary stopping place in the attack. A battalion would dig itself in at night—perhaps improve an ordinary water ditch with firing recesses—in the expectation of getting on a bit further the next day. The change and chance of war has caused these positions to become more or less

---

[4] **adversary**—enemy.

permanent and every day of rain has made them more and more unpleasant until now the chief question is how to keep the men more or less out of the water. In a summer campaign it would not matter, but when a hard frost sets in at night, and we have had several (luckily short) spells, frostbite sets in at once and the man is done for so far as his feet and legs are concerned. Our own British troops have stood it wonderfully well but some of the Indian regiments have suffered pretty severely in this respect. As you may well imagine some of these trenches that have been held for a long time are in a pretty grizzly state.

In the fight against the elements there was little energy to spare for fighting the enemy and, in any event, in such conditions attack was all but impossible. It was obvious that the Germans were in the same plight and on frosty nights, when the clouds cleared and the light from a hazy moon rippled on lagoons of ice and water spread across the **morass**,[5] when the machine-guns fell silent and only the occasional smack of a bullet cracked in the frosty air, the Tommies[6] could hear the splosh and thud of boots and spades in front and see the Germans silhouetted fifty yards away engaged on the same dreary task, bailing and digging, and doubtless cursing, just as they were themselves.

Day after day throughout the cheerless month of January, Corporal Alex Letyford recorded a terse catalog of miseries in the pocket diary he kept wrapped in oil-cloth to protect it from the wet.

---

[5] **morass**—swamp or marsh.

[6] Tommies—British soldiers.

Cpl. A. Letyford, 5th Field Coy., Royal Engineers.

1/1/15—At 6 P.M. (in dark) go to the trenches making culvert and dams. Trenches knee-deep in water. We work until 3 A.M.

2/1/15—6 P.M off to the trenches. I take some men and make dam to prevent water coming from German trench and return at 5 A.M.

3/1/15—Parade at 6 A.M. March to trenches. We dig communication trenches and are fired at the whole time. Work until 6 P.M.

4/1/15—During the day we build stables near billet[7] for our horses. At 6 P.M. we go to the lines and trace out redoubts.[8] Rather risky work as we are only eighty yards from the Germans who are doing a lot of sniping[9] from their lines. We also make a bridge across our front line. Four feet of water in this part of the trench line. Return to billets about midnight.

5/1/15—Spend the morning trying to dry out our clothes. We are all covered in mud from head to foot. At 6 P.M. I go with Captain Reed to the trenches and fix six pumps. Wading about in water to our waists until 2 A.M.

6/1/15—We go up at 8:45 A.M. and improve trenches for reserves.

7/1/15—Go out at 3 A.M. and make a bridge in the line of trenches about a hundred and fifty yards from Fritz. Return at daylight and rest remainder of day.

---

[7] billet—lodging for troops.

[8] redoubts—protected defensive areas.

[9] sniping—shooting at enemy forces from a concealed vantage point.

8/1/15—Again at work on the reserve trenches. At nightfall I remain with eight men and make the bridge again, it having been knocked into the stream. It rains nearly all the time and the enemy torment us with their Very lights and sniping. Return at 9 P.M.

9/1/15—Parade at 8 A.M. I take four men to dig communication trench. Work until 5 P.M. and reach billet at 6:30 P.M. The trenches are now waist-deep in water, part of section returned early, being soaked through, breast-high. My party had to run the gauntlet[10] on returning across the open in preference to coming through the trenches!

The journey was slow and hazardous, because it was impossible to accomplish it silently. The sound of splashing and sliding, the clink of tools, an inadvertent cry as a bridge collapsed or someone plunged into a water hole, were a sure sign that men were on the move, and the enemy flares would hiss into the sky, bathing the lines in **incandescent**[11] light that showed up every tree, every twig, every man who was caught in its glare. Then machine-guns would spit from their hidden posts and snipers take aim at such targets as they could see before the rocket burned out and plopped, sizzling, back to the sodden earth. It lasted seconds but, to the men standing motionless for fear of being spotted, it seemed an eternity.

Even quite far behind the front line it could be as dangerous by day, for the "line" was hardly a line at all, but a succession of outpost trenches cut off by the water-filled dykes that crisscrossed the flooded land. Under the cover of mist and darkness it was easy

---

[10] run the gauntlet—run between the opposing lines of armed men.
[11] **incandescent**—glowing with heat.

enough for snipers to slip through and find hideouts convenient for taking pot-shots at unsuspecting or unwary soldiers. In the lines themselves, marooned all day in barrels begged from breweries to provide reasonably dry standing, sentries kept a sharp look-out, but snipers were devious and some, more courageous and ingenious, were skilled in the arts of disguise and deceit. Stories of spies and snipers abounded—and some of them were true.

Lt. R. Macleod, V Bty., RHA, 2 Indian Cavalry Div.

We had a little spy hunt the other day. We shifted our billet to a new place. On going into the loft we discovered a little observation place very neatly made in the roof. There was a place where two tiles could be easily slid up, giving a very good view over part of the country. (The rest of the tiles being cemented down.) There was also a supply of provisions concealed up there. At the back of the house there is a large barn, apparently filled with straw. On examining the place it was found that the straw was hollow, and contained a small room with a passage leading to it through which a man could crawl. There was also another passage leading out to a trap-door very cunningly concealed under a heap of straw above a cow stall. No spy has been near the place since. We only discovered the presence of the room and passage by walking on top of the straw, and finding it giving way under our feet.

Major Elliot-Hill had an even more thrilling encounter:

I was riding along a quiet country road when I heard a report from a rifle. I dismounted, tied my horse to a tree, and had a good look round. Presently I saw what at home we would call a farm laborer working at a turnip clamp in a field. Keeping out of his sight I rode back to the farm house where we are billeted and borrowed some not-very-savory farm laborer's clothes. I went back on foot and started walking up the ploughed field towards him as if I was very interested in the straightness of the furrow, but I was actually more interested in my automatic revolver. When I got within reach of the fellow I tackled him. It was a fairly good struggle but I overpowered him and managed to march him back and hand him over to the authorities. They were not much inclined to take me seriously at first, but they locked him up anyway. They soon changed their tune when we went back to the turnip clamp and found a rifle and fifty rounds of ammunition hidden in it.

QUESTIONS TO CONSIDER

1. Why do the soldiers feel that the weather—rather than the Germans—is their chief enemy?

2. How would you describe Cpl. A. Letyford's attitude toward the war? Support your interpretation.

3. Why does Macdonald say that spades were the weapons needed most by soldiers involved in trench warfare?

Christmas, 1914

BY FRANK RICHARDS

Private Frank Richards wrote his account of the war in Old Soldiers Never Die. *In this excerpt he tells how British and German troops spent one Christmas, how the French people in the countryside reacted to it, and about some other difficulties of life in the trenches.*

CHRISTMAS, 1914

On Christmas morning we stuck up a board with "A Merry Christmas" on it. The enemy had stuck up a similar one. Platoons would sometimes go out for twenty-four hours rest—it was a day at least out of the trench and relieved the monotony a bit—and my platoon had gone out in this way the night before, but a few of us stayed behind to see what would happen. Two of our men then threw their equipment off and jumped on the **parapet**[1] with their hands above their heads. Two of the Germans did the same and commenced to walk up the river bank, our two men going to meet them. They met

---

[1] **parapet**—a wall or rampart of earth or stone to protect soldiers.

and shook hands and then we all got out of the trench. Buffalo Bill rushed into the trench and endeavoured to prevent it, but he was too late: the whole of the Company were now out, and so were the Germans. He had to accept the situation, so soon he and the other company officers climbed out too. We and the Germans met in the middle of no-man's-land. Their officers were also now out. Our officers exchanged greetings with them. One of the German officers said that he wished he had a camera to take a snapshot, but they were not allowed to carry cameras. Neither were our officers.

We mucked in all day with one another. They were Saxons and some of them could speak English. By the look of them their trenches were in as bad a state as our own. One of their men, speaking in English, mentioned that he had worked in Brighton for some years and that he was fed up to the neck with this damned war and would be glad when it was all over. We told him that he wasn't the only one that was fed up with it. We did not allow them in our trench and they did not allow us in theirs. The German Company-Commander asked Buffalo Bill if he would accept a couple of barrels of beer and assured him that they would not make his men drunk. They had plenty of it in the brewery. He accepted the offer with thanks and a couple of their men rolled the barrels over and we took them into our trench. The German officer sent one of his men back to the trench, who appeared shortly after carrying a tray with bottles and glasses on it. Officers of both sides clinked glasses and drunk one another's health. Buffalo Bill had presented them with a plum pudding just before. The officers came to an understanding that the unofficial truce would end at midnight. At dusk we went back to our respective trenches.

We had a decent Christmas dinner. Each man had a tin of Maconochie's and a decent portion of plum pudding. (A tin of Maconochie's consisted of meat, potatoes, beans and other vegetables and could be eaten cold, but we generally used to fry them up in the tin on a fire. I don't remember any man ever suffering from tin or lead poisoning through doing them in this way. The best firms that supplied them were Maconochie's and Moir Wilson's, and we could always depend on having a tasty dinner when we opened one of their tins. But another firm that supplied them at this time must have made enormous profits out of the British Government. Before ever we opened the first tins that were supplied by them we smelt a rat. The name of the firm made us suspicious. When we opened them our suspicions were well founded. There was nothing inside but a rotten piece of meat and some boiled rice. The head of that firm should have been put against the wall and shot for the way they sharked[2] us troops.) The two barrels of beer were drunk, and the German officer was right: if it was possible for a man to have drunk the two barrels himself he would have bursted before he had got drunk. French beer was rotten stuff.

Just before midnight we all made it up not to commence firing before they did. At night there was always plenty of firing by both sides if there were no working parties or patrols out. Mr. Richardson, a young officer who had just joined the Battalion and was now a platoon officer in my company, wrote a poem during the night about the Briton and the Bosche meeting in no-man's-land on Christmas day, which he read out to us. A few days later it was published in *The Times* or *Morning Post*, I believe. During the whole of Boxing Day[3] we never fired a shot, and they the same, each side seemed to be waiting for the other to set the ball a-rolling. One of their men shouted across in English

---

[2] sharked—tricked or cheated.

[3] Boxing Day—the first weekday after Christmas in Great Britain.

and inquired how we had enjoyed the beer. We shouted back and told him it was very weak but that we were very grateful for it. We were conversing off and on during the whole of the day. We were relieved that evening at dusk by a battalion of another brigade. We were mighty surprised as we had heard no whisper of any relief during the day. We told the men who relieved us how we had spent the last couple of days with the enemy, and they told us that by what they had been told the whole of the British troops in the line, with one or two exceptions, had mucked in with the enemy. They had only been out of action themselves forty-eight hours after being twenty-eight days in the front-line trenches. They also told us that the French people had heard how we had spent Christmas day and were saying all manner of nasty things about the British Army.

Going through Armentières that night some of the French women were standing in the doors spitting and shouting at us: "You no bon, you English soldiers, you boko kamerade Allemenge." We cursed them back until we were blue in the nose, and the Old Soldier, who had a wonderful command of bad language in many tongues, excelled himself. We went back to Erquinghem on the outskirts of Armentières and billeted in some sheds. Not far from the sheds was a large building which had been converted into a bath-house for the troops. We had our first bath one day in the latter end of November, and on the twenty-seventh of December we had our second. Women were employed in the bath-house to iron the seams of our trousers, and each man handed in his shirt, underpants and socks and received what were supposed to be clean ones in exchange; but in the seams of the shirts were the eggs, and after a man had his clean shirt on for a few hours the heat of his body would hatch them and he would be just as lousy[4]

---

[4] lousy—full of lice.

as ever he had been. I was very glad when I had that second bath, because I needed a pair of pants. A week before whilst out in the village one night I had had a scrounge through a house and found a magnificent pair of ladies' bloomers.[5] I thought it would be a good idea to discard my pants, which were skin-tight, and wear these instead, but I soon discovered that I had made a grave mistake. The crawlers, having more room to maneuver in, swarmed into those bloomers by platoons, and in a few days time I expect I was the lousiest man in the company. When I was stripping for the bath Duffy and the Old Soldier noticed the bloomers, and they both said that I looked sweet enough to be kissed.

---

[5] bloomers—loose undergarments, gathered at the knee, formerly worn by women or girls.

QUESTIONS TO CONSIDER

1. What does the behavior of the British and German soldiers on Christmas day reveal about their attitude toward each other and the war?

2. Why are the French angry with the British soldiers after the Christmas Day cease-fire?

3. How would you describe Frank Richards' attitude toward the enemy?

Stalemate and Attrition

BY PAUL FUSSELL

If war were a football game, then World War I was one in which the defense had such an advantage, no forward progress could be made. In The Norton Book of Modern War, *historian and critic Paul Fussell writes about how trench warfare made this so.*

Stalemate[1] and **attrition**[2] are terms inseparable from the memory of the First World War. Because massed, quick-firing artillery and machine guns employed by the thousands gave the defense an unprecedented advantage, both the Allies and the Central Powers found themselves virtual prisoners of their trenches for months on end. Indeed, from the winter of 1914 until the spring of 1918, the trench system seemed fixed, moving now and then a few hundred yards forward or back, on

---

[1] **stalemate**—a contest with no winners; a standoff.
[2] **attrition**—a gradual reduction of numbers or strength.

great occasions moving as much as a few miles. Theoretically it would have been possible to walk from the North Sea beaches all the way to the Alps entirely below ground, but actually the trench system was not absolutely continuous. It was broken here and there, with mere shell holes or fortified strong points serving as connecting links. A little more than half the Allied line was occupied by the French. The rest was British, consisting of about 800 battalions of some 1,000 men each. The two main concentrations of Allied strength were the Ypres Salient in Flanders[3] and the Somme[4] area in Picardy. . . .

Ideally, there were three parallel lines of trenches facing the enemy, with the front-line trench fifty yards to a mile or so from its hostile counterpart across the way. Several yards behind the front-line trench was the support trench, and several yards behind that the reserve. These were "firing" trenches, connected by communication trenches running perpendicular. "Saps," shallower trenches, ran out into No Man's Land, giving access to forward observation and listening posts, as well as grenade ("bomb") throwing positions and machine gun nests. Coming up to the trenches from the rear, you might walk in a communication trench a mile or more long. It often began in a town and gradually deepened, and by the time it reached the reserve trench it would be eight feet deep. Into the sides of the trenches were dug "funk holes," where one or two men would crouch when shelling became particularly heavy. There were also deep dugouts, reached by crude stairways, used as officers' quarters and command posts. The floor of a well-constructed trench was covered with wooden duckboards because the bottom of a trench was usually wet and the walls, always crumbling, had to be reinforced

---

[3] Flanders—Belgium.

[4] Somme—a river in Northern France.

by sandbags, corrugated iron, or bundles of reeds. A trench was protected on the enemy side by **copious**[5] entanglements of barbed wire, placed far enough out to prevent the enemy's crawling up to grenade-throwing range. The normal way of using the trenches was for a unit to occupy the front trench for a week or so, then, replaced by fresh men from the rear, to move back to the support trench, and so, after another week, to the reserve. Then perhaps a few days in a battered town way back, and then the sequence all over again. . . .

A day in a front-line trench . . . began about an hour before first light—say, 4:30. This was the moment for the invariable ritual of morning stand-to, when everyone stared across No Man's Land, weapon ready, and prepared to repel attack. After the dawn danger had passed, the men stood down and prepared breakfast in small groups, frying bacon and heating tea over small, preferably smokeless fires. In British trenches the daily rum ration of about two tablespoonsful was then doled out to each man. Before attacking, when the troops would have to climb out of the trench on ladders and cross No Man's Land, larger doses would be **vouchsafed.**[6] One medical officer deposed after the war was over, "Had it not been for the rum ration I do not think we should have won the war."

During the day everyone stayed below the top of the trench and cleaned weapons or repaired those parts of the trench damaged by the night's artillery fire. But when nighttime came the real work began. Wiring parties went out in front to repair the wire and to install new entanglements. Digging parties went forward in saps to extend them. Carrying parties negotiated the communication trenches, bringing up rations and

---

[5] **copious**—plentiful.

[6] **vouchsafed**—granted as a privilege or special favor.

ammunition and mail. All this night work was likely to be illuminated suddenly by enemy flares, and it was often interrupted by machine-gun and artillery fire. . . .

But now and then trench routine would be dramatically violated by an attempt at a large-scale advance. Most of these proved futile and disastrous, none more so than the battle of the Somme, which the British fought from July to November 1916. Planned meticulously for over six months—new railway lines were laid, masses of ammunition and supplies were laid in, a seven-to-one superiority in troops was assured, the German lines were deluged with a full week's artillery fire from over 1,500 guns—the Somme attack had every reason to succeed. At 7:30 on the morning of July 1, 1916, the attacking waves of eleven British divisions left their trenches and, filled with hope, began walking, their rifles at port arms, toward the German trenches. A minute later the machine-gun units of the six German divisions facing them carried their weapons upstairs from their deep dugouts and simply hosed down the attackers. One astonished German machine-gunner recalled, "We were very surprised to see them walking. We had never seen that before. . . . When we started firing we just had to load and reload. They went down in their hundreds. You didn't have to aim, we just fired into them." Of the 110,000 who attacked, 60,000 were killed or wounded before the day was over. More than 20,000 lay dead between the lines, and it was days before the wounded in No Man's Land stopped crying out. The failure of the attack seemed to **encapsulate**[7] all the bizarre **anomalies**[8] and frustrations of the First World War. Trying to make sense of the events of July 1, 1916, Edmund Blunden concluded that the stalemate

---

[7] **encapsulate**—to summarize or condense.

[8] **anomalies**—deviations or departures from the norm.

was hopeless, the war ridiculously **static,**[9] triumphal breakthrough impossible. "By the end of the day," he wrote, "both sides had seen, in a sad scrawl of broken earth and murdered men, the answer to the question. No road. No thoroughfare. Neither race had won, nor could win, the War. The War had won, and would go on winning."

---

[9] **static**—unmoving or unchanging; stalled.

QUESTIONS TO CONSIDER

1. Why did "stalemate and attrition" play a large part in trench warfare?

2. From the Allied standpoint, who or what was to blame for the Battle of the Somme disaster?

3. What did Edmund Blunden mean when he said, "The War had won, and would go on winning"?

Of Generals

BY A. J. P. TAYLOR

The historian Taylor, who often writes with a sense of what's funny about humans, is scathing in this bitter attack on the European generals who waged the early years of the war.

The political leaders added to the clamor, defining —or obscuring—the war aims of their countries in a cloud of words. It did not occur to them that there was anything else they could do. They had provided the armies; now they stood aside while the generals won the war for them. The French government virtually **abdicated**[1] in favour of Joffre, the commander-in-chief. The Chancellor of Germany regarded himself as the servant of the High Command.

In Great Britain Lord Kitchener, conqueror of the Sudan and of the Boers, became Secretary for War and ran the war almost single-handed. Only generals, it was felt, understood the art of war. Yet none of the generals

---

[1] **abdicated**—formally gave up power or responsibility.

except the British had any experience of war, and the British experiences against the Boers provided few useful lessons for the western front. The generals had acquired one skill only during the long years of peace: they knew how to move large numbers of men and horses by train. Once the men arrived at the railhead, their bodies were flung against the enemy in a tactic which had not changed since Napoleonic, or even Roman, times.

Army officers in every country came from the conservative privileged classes and had no contact with the scientific creative spirit of the age. When their first brutal onslaughts failed, they cried out for more men or, at most, for more shells. They did not cry out for new methods. No general consulted a civil engineer or the head of a great industrial concern, and the only general with a scientific training, the Australian, Sir John Monash, remained in a subordinate position until the end of the war. The generals had little interest in new weapons. They had accepted the rifle, though mainly in order to stick a bayonet on the end of it—a variant of the pike.[2] They resented the machine-gun as a defensive and therefore cowardly weapon. They regarded the tank and aeroplane with suspicion. They were even indifferent to motor transport for their men, though not for themselves. They sat in remote headquarters, working on railway-timetables and accumulating an ever greater weight of men and shells.

Weight was the only offensive idea in the first two years of the war—the only idea of Joffre and of Haig, who became British commander-in-chief in the autumn of 1915, and the only idea of Hindenburg and Ludendorff[3] on the eastern front. All acquired great public reputation from a record of failure. Machine-guns were effective

[2] pike—a long spear formerly used in combat.

[3] Hindenburg and Ludendorff were the top German commanders.

in stopping men. Earth, thrown up by the spade, was effective in stopping shells. Even if the occasional dent or gap were made, it could be closed by new defenders, who arrived by rail more rapidly than the attackers could plod forward on foot. Joffre's offensive in Champagne in 1915 and Haig's offensive on the Somme in 1916 hardly moved their respective lines forward at all. The Germans achieved a real breakthrough on the eastern front at Gorlice in May 1915 and were then defeated by their own weight; they could not move across the wastes of Russian Poland fast enough to prevent the Russians from forming a new defensive line. Verdun was the crowning symbol of this war. Its loss would have been no strategic disaster for the French; its capture would have brought no strategic gain for the Germans. Yet both sent soldiers through this mincing-machine by the hundred thousand, merely in order to batter against each other. Joffre openly announced that the war could be won only by **attrition**,[3] even if it meant killing three French and British for every two German soldiers. Sir William Robertson, Chief of the Imperial General Staff, approved and called this the principle of the longer purse.

---

[3] **attrition**—a gradual reduction of numbers or strength.

QUESTIONS TO CONSIDER

1. According to A. J. P. Taylor, what was the offensive strategy or plan of the first two years of the war?

2. Judging from this selection, what do you think angers Taylor the most about World War I?

3. What do you think is meant by the "principle of the longer purse"? Explain.

Technology and the War

Gas Warfare To protect himself and his transportation from the deadly effects of gas, both this cavalry officer and his horse have donned gas masks.

The Railway Gun This 14-inch railway gun, coordinated with airplane observations, pounds the enemy's lines from a distance of 20 miles.

▼

▲

Machine Guns The machine guns of World War I had increased firepower over those used in earlier European conflicts. A few could cause thousands of casualties. They were so effective against the infantry that the entire western front was under siege.

◀ **Incendiary Bomb** Various specialized projectiles were developed during the war. Shells were filled with magnesium and served as flares to light up the night battlefield. They were filled with chlorine or mustard gas to burn enemy troops. This is an incendiary bomb, designed to explode the hydrogen-filled zeppelins that were used, among other things, to bomb London.

Tanks: New Weapons of War With trench warfare, the old armored cars were no longer usable. Protected vehicles that could move over rough ground and across barbed wire were needed. So the tank that moved on its own tracks was developed. The British were the first to use them in the Battle of the Somme in 1916. These are American tanks going toward the battle line in the Forest of Argonne in October 1918. ▶

Submarines World War I was the first war in which submarines became a major factor. Germans first used them to fire torpedoes at vessels carrying supplies to the enemy. The drowning of American passengers on several torpedoed ships helped propel the United States into the war.
▼

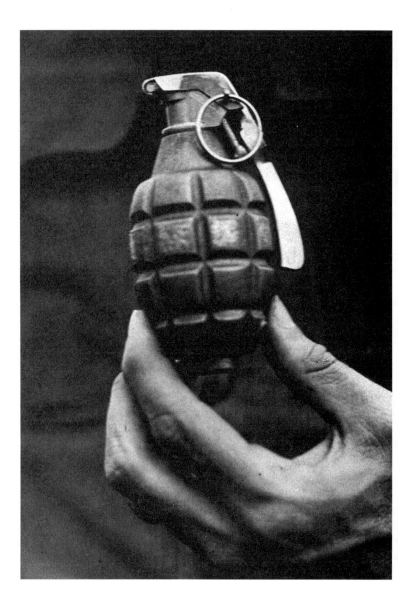

◀ **Hand Grenades** The hand grenade was so effective in trench warfare that it became a standard piece of infantry equipment. Small explosives like the one shown here could be held in the hand and thrown at close range.

Radio Communications Radio was the vital link between the troops and guns on the ground and the observation planes in the sky.
▼

War in the Air

BY JAMES CAMERON

*Rumors and enthusiasm greeted the beginnings of air warfare.
This was the first time planes had been used in battle, and the
public, encouraged by a press that was more a propaganda arm
of each nation than an objective reporter, was by turns thrilled
and frightened. In this excerpt from his book 1914, a British writer
describes the early years.*

Overhead there developed a phenomenon that itself
marked out this war from any other: men were fighting
in the air. One grew accustomed to the spectacle, as
one grew accustomed to so many unprecedented and
generally sinister things; nevertheless it had never sig-
nificantly happened before.

To begin with the aeroplane was an erratic toy, most
effectively used as a scout, an artillery spotter or observer,
flying low among the rifle-bullets and returning to base
with news of the enemy dispositions. Sometimes it was
more ambitious. Quite early in October the Admiralty
announced that there had been "an aerial invasion of

Germany by British aviators." Squadron-Commander Spencer Grey RN with two lieutenants had flown to Düsseldorf and thrown several bombs on an aircraft shed, setting a Zeppelin dirigible[1] on fire. "The feat," said the Admiralty, "would appear to be in every way remarkable, having regard to the distance—over one hundred miles—penetrated into enemy territory."

It was only some two months, after all, since the Norwegian Lieutenant Trygve Gran had made the first historic crossing of the North Sea by aeroplane.

Three days later the Germans replied by sending two Taubes over Paris. They dropped small bombs around the Opera, in the rue Montmartre, rue Lafayette, rue de la Banque, the place de la Republique. Three people were killed. One bomb fell on the terrace of Notre Dame, but it bounced away without exploding.

The coastal towns of Dunkirk and Calais saw a German plane every day, so regularly that "half past three" was known as "Taube et demie." It would appear, drop a bomb or two, break some glass, kill one or two people, and go away.

Over the line itself the aeroplanes met in single combat or in groups, and the science of aerial battle was born. In the skies of northern France Fokkers met Farmans, Sopwiths met Taubes, roaring little instruments of fretwork and piano-wire; there among the clouds they maneuvered like terriers, weaving and circling at seventy and even eighty miles an hour. It was greatly improvised—the aviators actually duelled with rifles, or even pistols; sometimes a carbine[2] was fixed by an attachment to the side of the cockpit where the pilot could reach it. . . .

---

[1] Zeppelin dirigible—an airship with a long, cylindrical body, supported by gas cells.

[2] carbine—a lightweight rifle with a short barrel.

The first **echelon**[3] of the Royal Flying Corps had not been slow to move into action; it had embarked from Southampton on 11th August, for its forward base at Amiens, under the command of Brigadier General Sir David Henderson, Director of Military Aeronautics, the first man to lead an aerial force into a major war. He had, to begin with, a total uniformed strength of his RFC of 2,073 men. He had an organization only two years old, and 130 aeroplanes. (France had 500, Germany 470, even Austria had 120. Germany was known also to have two dozen important lighter-than-air flying machines, of which some twenty were to the design of the Graf Zeppelin; they were unknown quantities.)

The observer of one Naval aeroplane won a momentary renown by effecting the extraordinary feat of changing a propeller-blade two thousand feet above the Channel.

From time to time spies were deposited behind the enemy lines on both sides, and, less frequently, collected. An increase in aerial activity generally revived the stories, always current among the ground troops, of enemy agents in their midst. Somebody had recalled what Frederick the Great said: "When Marshal Soubise goes to war he is followed by a hundred cooks—when I take the field I am preceded by a hundred spies." In the forward areas of northern France agents were thought, perhaps rightly, to abound—flashing lights at night, emitting puffs of smoke by day, affecting to be laborers working the fields, disguised as refugees, above all making use of church towers, the hands of whose clocks they could manipulate as semaphores.[4]

---

[3] **echelon**—a formation of groups, units, or individuals.

[4] semaphores—visual signals.

The German aircraft were often held to be a more mobile and **impudent**[5] version of the same thing, and whenever a Taube was intercepted overhead the ensuing dog-fight was watched with huge partisan enthusiasm.

[5] **impudent**—cocky and bold.

QUESTIONS TO CONSIDER

1. How were airplanes used during World War I?

2. Based on this selection, do you think World War I was won in the skies or on the ground? Explain your answer.

Ace of the Iron Cross

BY ERNST UDET

Second only to Baron Manfred von Richthofen, the famous Red Baron, the author of this piece was Germany's best pilot. He held the rank of Oberleutnant in the Imperial German Air Service. After the war he wrote his memoirs, and the English translation was published under the title Ace of the Iron Cross. *A successful fighter pilot was known as an "ace," and the Iron Cross was the highest medal the German government awarded its military heroes. Here, from a chapter called "First Combats," Udet recalls overcoming cowardice.*

The Single-Seater Combat Command Habsheim consists of four pilots. Lieutenant Pfaelzer is the C.O. [Commanding Officer], and besides me there are Sergeant Weingaertner and Corporal Glinkermann. We are all young people and live like princes in the vacant villa of a rich American who fled at the outset of the war.

A pleasant tone prevails among the men of the command. Weingaertner and I soon become friends. This is one of the things about Weingaertner. By the third day of acquaintance everyone befriends him.

Glinkermann is more difficult and remote. In the evening, he often sits with the mechanics, smoking his pipe and staring into the fog, which rises from the meadows in white clouds. I think he is quite poor and very much depressed about it. Much later, when his wallet is brought to me, I find a picture of a girl riding at the head of a laughing **cavalcade.**[1] He had never spoken about it. Some **jibe**[2] at him when he comes along with the wrappings of his leggings in perpetual disarray with a bit of white from his long johns showing through. But he is a good flier, one of the best I've known.

Duty is easy and comfortable. Once or twice a day we take off to fly cover for about an hour. But we hardly ever see the enemy. The December sky is cold and clear, the earth brittle with frost. If one wraps up well and butters the face, flying is a pleasure. Almost like a sleigh ride on the clouds.

Up in Flanders and in Champagne, where there is fighting and pilots are falling daily on both sides, they speak of the sleeping armies in the Vosges. It is said a little **disparagingly,**[3] touched with envy.

One morning the alarm sounds quite early. This is unusual. The forward observers report that a Caudron has passed over the lines and is heading in our direction. I climb into my crate and take off. The clouds hang low, a ceiling of barely four hundred meters. I push into the gray haze and climb higher and higher.

At two thousand meters a blue sky arches above me, with a strangely pale December sun shining down. I look around. Far back in the west, above the carpet of the clouds, I see a small dot, like a ship cruising on the horizon of the sea—the Caudron. I head straight for him, and he continues to come toward me. We close

---

[1] **cavalcade**—a procession.

[2] **jibe**—heckle, sneer, or tease.

[3] **disparagingly**—in a belittling, slighting way.

quickly. I can already recognize the wide wing span, the two motors, and the **gondola**[4] hanging, narrow like the body of a bird of prey, between the wings. We are at the same altitude, going toward each other. This is against all the rules, because the Caudron is an observation plane, but I am a fighter. Pressing the button on my stick would send a stream of bullets belching from my machine gun, sufficient to tear him up in the air. He must know this as well as I. Just the same, he continues straight toward me.

He is now so close, I can make out the head of the observer. With his square goggles he looks like a giant, malevolent insect coming toward me to kill. The moment has come when I must fire. But I can't. It is as though horror has frozen the blood in my veins, paralyzed my arms, and torn all thought from my brain with the swipe of a paw. I sit there, flying on, and continue to stare, as though mesmerized, at the Caudron now to my left. Then the machine gun barks across to me. The impacts on my Fokker sound like metallic clicks. A tremor runs through my machine, a solid whack on my cheek, and my goggles are torn off. I reach up instinctively. Fragments, glass splinters from my goggles. My hand is wet with blood.

I push the stick, nose down, and dive into the clouds. I'm benumbed. How did this happen, how was it possible?

"You were timid, you were a coward," hammers the motor. And then, only one thought: "Thank God, no one saw this!"

The flowing green, the pine tops, the airfield. I land. The mechanics come running. I don't wait for them. I climb out of the cockpit and head for the quarters. The medic removes the glass splinters with a pair of tweezers.

---

[4] **gondola**—elongated car attached to the underside of an airplane.

They had bored into the flesh around my eyes. It should hurt, but I don't feel a thing.

Then I go up to my room and throw myself onto my bed. I want to sleep, but my thoughts return over and over, allowing no relaxation. Is it cowardice when one fails in the first moment of combat? I want to calm myself and say: "Nerves—it can happen to anyone. Next time you'll do better!" But my conscience refuses to be satisfied with such an easy declaration. It presents me with the hard fact: You failed, because in the moment of combat you thought of yourself, you were afraid for your life. At this moment I recognize the meaning of soldiering.

To be a soldier means to think of the enemy and of victory and to forget one's self in the process! It is possible that the line of **demarcation**[5] between the man and the coward is narrow as the edge of a sword. But he who would remain a man among men must, at the moment of decision, have the strength to choke off the animal fear within himself, because the animal within ourselves wants to live at any price. And he who gives in to it will forever be lost to the fraternity of men where honor, duty, and belief in the Fatherland is the **credo.**[6]

I step to the window and look down. Weingaertner and Glinkermann are walking up and down in front of the house. Perhaps they never had to face up to it as I just did, and I promise myself that from this moment on I will be nothing but a soldier. I will shoot straighter and fly better than my comrades until I have wiped out the blot against my honor.

Together with Behrend, who has followed me to Habsheim, I go to work. We make a silhouette model of a Nieuport, as it would be seen from behind during an attack. Evenings, when flying activities have come to an

[5] **demarcation**—boundary or separation.
[6] **credo**—creed; a set of fundamental beliefs.

end, I set up the target in the middle of the airfield. From three hundred meters I dive down, and at one hundred meters I open fire. I pull out at a very low altitude and climb again, and the game begins anew. Behrend has to count the hits, and he signals to me. Hits in the motor count double, and ten hits mean a glass of beer for him. Often I have stoppages—too often. Behrend and I often work late into the night to eliminate these malfunctions.

Then the results improve. Actually, they improve surprisingly fast. I'm quite happy until I discover that Behrend helps with the pencil. Out of friendship for me, he claims, but I think it's for his love of beer.

Orders come down that ammunition is to be conserved, so I have to cut down on my practice flights. By way of compensation, however, we now frequently attack the French trenches from the air.

One evening, on one of these trench flights, I am a bit behind schedule. It is up north, close to Thaun. The enemy machine gun nests, bedded and hidden in pine forests, have proved tempting targets. By the time I fly back to the airstrip, night has fallen.

Below, they light pitch torches to guide me home. Their reddish glow flickers across the field, giving a diffuse and restless illumination. I line up for the landing. It is difficult to see the ground. I touch down hard enough to damage the undercarriage. Otherwise the machine is fine, but I will be out of action for a day at least.

I tell Behrend and the other mechanic I want them out on the field at four-thirty the next morning. Behrend pulls a face. The next day is a Sunday, and when Behrend is expected to work on Sundays he suddenly becomes religious.

The lead gray of the morning light lies on the airfield as we begin our work. The woods stand about us like a darkly threatening **phalanx**.[7] The bare wooden walls of the small **hangars**[8] reflect a pale light. A peculiar mood prevails, as though something extraordinary were in the air. I'm not sure whether it will mean good or bad luck.

At six, the church bells in the surrounding towns begin to chime, and their sound drifts over to us across the treetops. The sun has risen, and we continue to work silently. It has gotten so warm, we sweat even though we are wearing only our blue work jackets. At twelve noon we finish. Behrend and his buddy make a fast getaway; they still want to catch the train to Muelhausen.

It is quiet now, everyone has gone to town on pass. I drive to our quarters and eat lunch. I have the table all to myself and have the coffee brought to me out in the garden. There, I sit in a field chair smoking and stare into the sky.

At three-thirty a telephone operator comes running with a report from the observers in the forward trenches: Two French aircraft have passed over the lines and are rapidly approaching Altkirch.

I jump into the car and go tearing off to the airfield. Without thinking, instinct tells me with certainty: This is it! The machine is ready to start, and mechanics are standing around. The telephone operator had had enough presence of mind to rouse everyone still on the base. I climb into the cockpit and take off.

I claw my way up in the direction of the front lines. I must try to gain superior height so I might have the edge in the flight. Twenty-eight hundred meters . . . I fly west toward Altkirch. Just as I am above Altkirch, I see them. I count: One . . . two . . . three . . . four . . . I reach up to wipe my goggles . . . this is impossible, it can't be! Those black dots must be oil flecks, spray from the

---

[7] **phalanx**—group of armed soldiers.

[8] **hangars**—covered shelters used for housing and repairing aircraft.

motor. But no, the dots remain, and they grow larger. Seven, I count, seven in a row, and beyond them another wave appears, again five and again . . . they are coming closer, sharply silhouetted against the yellow silken flush of the afternoon sky. Twenty-two of them, bombers of the Caudron and Farman types. They come buzzing on like a swarm of angry hornets, pell-mell, without any discernible formation. High above the others glides the queen of the swarm, a mighty Voisin. I pull at the stick. We are closing fast. They certainly must have taken notice of me, but they act as though I don't exist. They don't climb a single centimeter and hold steadily to their course, east-northeast toward Muelhausen. I look around. The blue shell of the sky behind me is empty. None of my buddies from Habsheim have taken off. I am alone.

I reach them near Burnhaupt. Three hundred meters above them I make a wide turn and fall in with them on the course toward Muelhausen. I lean overboard to look at the gaggle of twenty-three machines, in the center a giant Farman. Between their wings I see bits of the ground, blue slate roofs, red tile. This is it! My heart is beating in my throat. My hands, grabbing the stick, are damp. One against twenty-three!

My Fokker flits above the gaggle like a hound chasing the boar. He pursues him—but he doesn't attack. At this moment I know: If this second passes without a fight, then it's good-bye fighter piloting for me. I will have no recourse but to request a transfer away from the command.

We are over Dornbach, closely before Muelhausen. In the coffee gardens of the inns are people, colored flecks in the green-brown of the landscape. They are running back and forth, gesticulating and pointing up.

Then I clear the hurdle. From this instant on I see only one thing: That big Farman in the middle of the formation. I nose down, gather speed, and dive at full throttle. The enemy aircraft grows in front of me, becoming larger as though he were being hastily focused in a microscope. The observer stands up. I can see his round leather helmet. He whips up his machine gun and points it at me.

At eighty meters I want to fire, but I must be absolutely certain. Closer, closer, forty meters, thirty, now! Whatever the barrel will spit out . . . tack . . . tack . . . tack. There, he totters. A blue flame shoots from his exhaust, he lists, and white smoke belches forth—hit, hit in the gas tank!

Clack . . . clack . . . clack—with metallic sounds bullets hit my machine just in front of the cockpit. I whip my head around and look to the rear. Two Caudrons covering me with machine gun bursts. I remain calm. This will be done just as during the practice sessions at the airfield. Stick forward, and I dive down. Three hundred meters below I pull out.

The **fuselage**[9] of the Farman dives down past me like a giant torch, trailing a black cloud from which bright flames spurt forth. A man, his arms and legs spread out like a frog's, falls past—the observer.

At the moment, I don't think of them as human beings. I feel only one thing: Victory, triumph, victory! The iron vise about my breast has burst, and the blood courses through my body in mighty, free spurts.

The air above me is now filled with the thundering organ of the motors. In between, the hasty barking of the machine guns. All available machines have now risen from Habsheim and thrown themselves upon the enemy. Under the violence of their impact, the French squadron has broken up, and a number of single combats have ensued. Wherever one looks, there are machines twisting about in **dogfights**.[10]

---

[9] **fuselage**—the central body of an aircraft.
[10] **dogfights**—aerial battles between fighter planes.

A single Caudron is making a hasty exit to the west. He's not being followed. I chase after him at full throttle. The intoxication of the first fight has passed. The destruction of the enemy has become a tactical problem, nothing more.

I open fire at 150 meters and stop again. Too far, much too far. At eighty meters I let go with the second burst. This time I can clearly observe the effect. The Caudron trembles, the right engine puffs a small cloud of smoke, the prop slows up and stops. The pilot turns around and sees me. In a moment he goes down into a steep dive.

I stay with him. He's flying with only one engine; he can't get away from me. I am now so close to him I can feel his propwash.

A new burst—the pilot collapses on his stick. Then—stoppage! During the steep dive, the cartridges have loosened in the belt. I hammer at the gun with both fists. No good, it remains silent.

Out of action, I have no choice but to leave my opponent and return home. At five-twenty-five I land on the airfield at Habsheim. I had taken off at four-sixteen. The entire play has reeled off in an hour.

In the middle of the airstrip stands Captain Mackenthun, the C.O. of Habsheim Base. He stands straddle-legged, binoculars to the eyes, watching the fighting. I walk toward him: "Sergeant Udet returned from **sortie**.[11] Farman two-seater brought down!" He takes the binoculars down and looks at me, his face emotionless, as though frozen in position. "Our large plane has just crashed over Napoleon's Island," he says.

I know that Lieutenant Kurth was the pilot and Mackenthun's best friend. I salute and walk toward the hangars.

---

[11] **sortie**—a flight of a combat aircraft on a mission.

Not until evening can we sort out the events of the day.

The French air attack, the first large-scale air attack ever on Germany, has been beaten off. Five enemy machines have been brought down on our side of the lines. Of the nine officers of one unit, who had started at noon, only three return. *"Tu finiras aussi à l'Île Napoléon!"*[12] has become the slogan when one wants to undertake a daring coup.

Three of our own men did not return: Kurth, Hopfgarten, and Wallat, the crew of the AEG G-type aircraft from the 48th Abteilung. They had attacked a Farman, were rammed during the dogfight, and the two went down in a ball of wreckage, just above Napoleon's Island. It happened on March 18, 1916.

In our villa in Habsheim, the windows remain lit up until late into the night. Men were killed on this day, but this time we were not merely along for the ride. Pfaelzer, Weingaertner, Glinkermann, and I each got his man.

We are young, and we celebrate our victory.

---

[12] *Tu finiras aussi à l'Île Napoléon!*—You will also end at Napoleon's Island.

QUESTIONS TO CONSIDER

1. Why doesn't Udet fire on the enemy Caudron during the early morning mission?

2. What does Udet do to help restore his nerve at the throttle?

3. What is Udet's definition of a soldier?

4. How does Udet feel during the dogfight over Muelhausen?

Snoopy and the Red Baron

BY CHARLES SCHULZ

The famous comic strip Peanuts *involves the activities of Charlie Brown and his friends, their sisters and brothers, and his dog Snoopy. Snoopy lives in a doghouse in the backyard. He can often be found lying on its steeply pitched roof, daydreaming. Among his favorite fantasies are his daring adventures as a World War I ace pilot, where he pits his courage against the fiercest fighter of them all, Baron Manfred von Richthofen, the Red Baron.*

Peanuts reprinted by permission of United Feature Syndicate, Inc.

Peanuts reprinted by permission of United Feature Syndicate, Inc.

QUESTIONS TO CONSIDER

1. What does Snoopy seem to admire most about the World War I fighter pilots?

2. Charles Schulz has been criticized by some for "glorifying" war in his *Peanuts* comic strips about the Red Baron. Do you agree with this criticism? Explain why or why not.

The Aviators

◀ **The Red Baron** Baron Manfred von Richthofen (1892–1918) was Germany's top aviator. A military man from 1912 on, he joined the Imperial Air Service in 1916. He became commander of Fighter Group 1, which was known as the "Flying Circus" because of the painted decorations on its planes. He personally brought down 80 enemy aircraft during his service. He was killed when his red Fokker triplane was fired on in a battle near Amiens, France.

Eddie Rickenbacker Captain Eddie Rickenbacker (1890–1973) was the United States' leading air ace. When war broke out, he was one of the country's top race-car drivers. Assigned to the 94th Aero Pursuit Squadron, he racked up 26 air victories and was awarded numerous awards, including the Congressional Medal of Honor.

▼

◄ American aviators read while waiting for the "alerte" which calls them to battle in the skies over France.

Insignia of the 96th Aero Squadron.
▼

Air Reconnaissance Major J. N. Reynolds of the 91st Aero Squadron
is unloading a camera he used to take photographs at 25,000 feet.
▼

▲

A Downed German Plane German prisoners are being used to camouflage this plane after it was shot down over France.

from

The Ghost Road

BY PAT BARKER

The Ghost Road *won Great Britain's highest literary award, the* Booker Prize. *The third book in a trilogy about World War I, it is a bitter, tragic story of the war's final days in 1918. Billy Prior, the character whose diary entries make up this excerpt, has suffered a mental breakdown earlier in the war. Now recovered, he has returned to France to fight, though he now no longer believes in the war.*

27 October—Everybody finds these marches gruelling. I spend a lot of my time on foot inspections. Some of the men have blisters the size of eggs. And my own feet, which were not good this morning, are now very not good.

But we're in decent billets[1] tonight. I've actually got a bed in a room with roses on the wallpaper, and a few left in the garden too. Went out and picked some and put

---

[1] billets—lodgings for soldiers.

them in a bowl on the kitchen table in memory of Amiens. Big blowsy roses well past their best, but we move on again today so I won't be here to see the petals fall.

29 October—Arrived here under cover of darkness. Village wretched, people unsmiling, dazed-looking, not surprising when you think we were bombing them to buggery not long ago.

There's a rumor going round that the Austrians have signed a peace treaty. The men cheered up when they heard it, and they need cheering when you look at their feet. Nobody here can understand why it's still going on.

I lay in bed last night and listened to them in the barn singing. I wish I didn't feel they're being sacrificed to the subclauses and the small print. But I think they are.

Thursday, 31 October—And here for a while we shall stay. The Germans are dug in on the other side of the Sambre-Oise Canal, and seem to be preparing to make a stand.

The village is still occupied, but houses in the forward area have been evacuated and we're crammed into the cellar of one of them. Now and then we venture upstairs into the furnished rooms, feeling like rats or mice, and then we scurry back into our hole again. But it's warm, it feels safe, though the whole house shakes with the impact of exploding shells, and it's not good to think what a direct hit would do. Above ground the Germans have chopped down all the trees, but there's a great tangle of undergrowth, brambles that catch at your legs as you walk past, dead **bracken**[2] the exact shade, or one of the shades, of Sarah's[3] hair. No possibility of exercises or drill or anything. We lie low by day, and patrol at night, for of course they've left alarm posts on this side of the canal, a sort of human trip-wire to

---

[2] **bracken**—a widespread, weedy fern.
[3] Sarah's—reference to Prior's girlfriend.

warn of an impending attack. Cleaning them out's a nasty job since it has to be silent. Knives and knobkerries[4] in other words.

1 November—My turn to go out last night. One alarm post "exterminated." I hope it's the last. We crawled almost to the edge of the canal, and lay looking at it. There was just enough starlight to see by. A strong sense of the Germans on the other side, peering into the darkness as we were, silent, watchful. I had the sense that somewhere out there was a pair of eyes looking directly into mine.

The canal's raised about four feet above the surrounding fields, with drainage ditches on either side (the Germans have very sensibly flooded them). It's forty feet wide. Too wide to be easily bridged, too narrow from the point of view of a successful bombardment. There's no safety margin to allow for shells falling short, so men and equipment will have to be kept quite a long way back. Which means that when the barrage lifts, as it's supposed to do, and sweeps forward three hundred yards, there'll be about five minutes in which to get across the swampy fields, across the drainage ditches, and reach even our side of the canal. Plenty of time for them to get their breath and man the guns—though officially, of course, they'll all have been wiped out.

The field opposite's partially flooded already, and it's still raining. Not just rain, they've also flooded the drainage ditches on their side. From the canal the ground rises steeply to La Motte Farm, which is our objective in the attack. Uphill all the way. Not a scrap of cover. Machine-gunners behind every clump of grass.

Looking at the ground, even like that in semi-darkness, the problem became dreadfully apparent. Far clearer than it is on any of the maps, though we spend

---

[4] knobkerries—short, heavy wooden clubs used for striking or throwing.

hours of every day bent over them. There are two possibilities. Either you bombard the opposite bank so heavily that no machine-gunner can possibly survive, in which case the ditches and quite possibly even the canal bank will burst, and the field on the other side will become a nightmare of weltering mud ten feet deep, as bad as anything at Passchendaele. Or you keep the bombardment light, move it on quickly, and wait for the infantry to catch up. In that case you take the risk that unscathed machine-gunners will pop up all over the place, and settle down for a nice bit of concentrated target practice.

It's a choice between Passchendaele and the Somme.[5] Only a miniature version of each, but then that's not much consolation. It only takes one bullet per man.

They've chosen the Somme. This afternoon we had a joint briefing with the Lancashire Fusiliers on our left. Marshall-of-the-Ten-Wounds[6] was there, surprisingly outspoken I thought, though you can afford to be when you're so covered in wound stripes and medals it's starting to look like an eccentric form of camouflage. He said his men stand no chance of getting up the slope with machine-guns still intact above them and no cover. Building a bridge in the open under the sort of fire we're likely to encounter is impossible. The whole operation's insane. The chances of success are zero.

Nobody argued with him, I mean nobody discussed it. We were just told flatly, a simple, unsupported assertion, that the weight of the artillery would overcome all opposition. I think those words sent a chill down the spine of every man there who remembered the Somme. Marshall threw his pencil down and sat with his arms

---

[5] The Battle of the Somme (1916) lasted five months and ended when the Allies attempted to advance and were slaughtered by German machine-gun fire.

[6] Marshall-of-the-Ten-Wounds—the acting Lieutenant Colonel.

folded, silent, for the rest of the briefing.

So here we sit writing letters. Supplies take a long time to get here, because the Germans blocked the roads and blew up the bridges as they withdrew. Nobody's been inside a proper shop for six weeks, so I keep tearing pages out of the back of this book and giving them to people.

Not many left now. But enough.

QUESTIONS TO CONSIDER

1. What does Billy Prior mean when he says, "They've chosen the Somme"?

2. Which words and sentences in these diary entries reveal Prior's feelings about the war and those who are running it?

3. What is the significance of the final line of the selection?

War Poems

The poems that came out of World War I were not hymns of praise for heroic deeds. They were expressions of hopelessness and senselessness. They speak to sadness, loss, and the idiocy of it all. Here are a few short samples.

We're Here Because We're Here

BY ORDINARY BRITISH SOLDIERS

"We're Here Because We're Here" is a song sung by soldiers to the tune of "Auld Lang Syne." It is just the same lyrics over and over, saying there is no reason to be fighting this war.

We're here because we're here,
Because we're here, Because we're here.
We're here because we're here,
Because we're here, Because we're here.
Oh, here we are, oh, here we are,
Oh, here we are again.
Oh, here we are, oh, here we are,
Oh, here we are again.

Verses V and VI

BY E.E. CUMMINGS

*Verses V and VI, from a longer poem about the war entitled "Two,"
are by the American poet E. E. Cummings (1913–1962). He
makes the most ordinary conversational phrases have the tragic
power of poetry. Notice how enormously sad these few lines are.*

V

look at this)
a 75 done
this nobody would
have believed
would they no
kidding this was my particular

pal
funny aint
it we was
buddies
i used to

know
him lift the
poor cuss
tenderly this side up handle

with care
fragile
and send him home

to his old mother in
a new nice pine box

(collect

VI

first Jock he
was kilt a handsome
man and James and
next let me
see yes Will that was
cleverest
he was kilt and my youngest
boy was kilt last with
the big eyes i loved like you can't
imagine Harry was o
god kilt he was kilt everybody was kilt

they called them the kilties

Back

BY WILFRID GIBSON

British poet Wilfrid Gibson (1878–1962) explains why a returning soldier can't talk about the war.

They ask me where I've been,
And what I've done and seen.
But what can I reply
Who know it wasn't I,
But someone just like me,
Who went across the sea
And with my head and hands
Killed men in foreign lands . . .
Though I must bear the blame,
Because he bore my name.

High Wood

BY PHILIP JOHNSTONE

In "High Wood," Philip Johnstone imagines what might be said about a battlefield when it becomes just another tourist attraction.

Ladies and gentlemen, this is High Wood,
Called by the French, Bois des Fourneaux,
The famous spot which in Nineteen-Sixteen,
July, August and September was the scene
Of long and bitterly contested strife,

By reason of its High commanding site.
Observe the effect of shell-fire in the trees
Standing and fallen; here is wire; this trench
For months inhabited, twelve times changed hands;
(They soon fall in), used later as a grave.
It has been said on good authority
That in the fighting for this patch of wood
Were killed somewhere above eight thousand men,
Of whom the greater part were buried here,
This mound on which you stand being . . .
                    Madame, please,

You are requested kindly not to touch
Or take away the Company's property
As souvenirs; you'll find we have on sale
A large variety, all guaranteed.
As I was saying, all is as it was,
This is an unknown British officer,
The tunic having lately rotted off.
Please follow me—this way . . .
            the *path*, sir, *please,*

The ground which was secured at great expense
The Company keeps absolutely untouched,
And in that dug-out (genuine) we provide
Refreshments at a reasonable rate.
You are requested not to leave about
Paper, or ginger-beer bottles, or orange-peel,
There are waste-paper baskets at the gate.

QUESTIONS TO CONSIDER

1. What do you think the soldiers mean when they say, "We're here because we're here"?

2. In verse V of Cummings's poem, who is talking? How do you know? Who is talking in verse VI? Explain your answer.

3. In "Back," why does the returning soldier find that he can't talk about the war?

4. What effect does Johnstone create by alternating descriptions of the battlefield's history with comments to imaginary tourists?

America in the War

Address to Congress, April 1917

BY PRESIDENT WOODROW WILSON

*President Wilson was at heart a peacemaker. He tried repeatedly
throughout 1916 to bring the warring powers to accept "peace
without victory." He ran for his second term on a platform that
promised to keep the United States out of the war. In January,
1917, however, Germany announced it would begin unrestricted
submarine warfare against Britain and attack any ship, Allied or
neutral, going to Allied ports. In the following speech, Wilson asks
Congress to declare war on Germany, which it did on April 6.*

I have called the Congress into extraordinary session
because there are serious, very serious choices of policy
to be made, and made immediately, which it was neither
right nor constitutionally permissible that I should
assume the responsibility of making.

On the third of February last I officially laid before
you the extraordinary announcement of the Imperial
German Government that on and after the first day of

February it was its purpose to put aside all restraints of law or of humanity and use its submarines to sink every vessel that sought to approach either the ports of Great Britain and Ireland or the western coasts of Europe or any of the ports controlled by the enemies of Germany within the Mediterranean. . . .

I was for a little while unable to believe that such things would in fact be done by any government that had hitherto subscribed to the humane practices of civilized nations. International law had its origin in the attempt to set up some law which would be respected and observed upon the seas, where no nation had right of dominion and where lay the free highways of the world. . . . This minimum of right the German Government has swept aside under the plea of retaliation and necessity and because it had no weapons which it could use at sea except these which it is impossible to employ as it is employing them without throwing to the winds all scruples of humanity or of respect for all understandings that were supposed to underlie the intercourse of the world. I am not now thinking of the loss of property involved, immense and serious as that is, but only of the wanton and wholesale destruction of the lives of non-combatants, men, women, and children, engaged in pursuits which have always, even in the darkest periods of modern history, been deemed innocent and legitimate. Property can be paid for; the lives of peaceful and innocent people cannot be. The present German submarine warfare against commerce is a warfare against mankind.

It is a war against all nations. American ships have been sunk, American lives taken, in ways which it has stirred us very deeply to learn of, but the ships and people of other neutral and friendly nations have been sunk and overwhelmed in the waters in the way. There has been no discrimination. The challenge is to all mankind. Each nation must decide for itself how it will meet it. The choice we make for ourselves must be made with a moderation of counsel and a temperateness of judgment befitting our character and our motives as a nation. We must put excited feeling away. Our motive will not be revenge or the victorious assertion of the physical might of the nation, but only the vindication of right, of human right, of which we are only a single champion. . . .

With a profound sense of the solemn and even tragical character of the step I am taking and of the grave responsibilities which it involves, but in unhesitating obedience to what I deem my constitutional duty, I advise that the Congress declare the recent course of the Imperial German Government to be in fact nothing less than war against the government and people of the United States; that it formally accept the status of **belligerent**[1] which has thus been thrust upon it; and that it take immediate steps not only to put the country in a more thorough state of defense but also to exert all its power and employ all its resources to bring the Government of the German Empire to terms and end the war. . . .

We have no quarrel with the German people. We have no feeling towards them but one of sympathy and friendship. It was not upon their impulse that their government acted in entering this war. It was not with their previous knowledge or approval. It was a war determined upon as wars used to be determined upon in the old, unhappy days when peoples were nowhere consulted by their rulers and wars were provoked and waged in the interest of dynasties or of little groups of ambitious men who were accustomed to use their fellow men as pawns and tools. . . .

We are accepting this challenge of hostile purpose because we know that in such a Government, following

---

[1] **belligerent**—a nation at war.

such methods, we can never have a friend; and that in the presence of its organized power, always lying in wait to accomplish we know not what purpose, there can be no assured security for the democratic Governments of the world. We are now about to accept gauge of battle with this natural foe to liberty and shall, if necessary, spend the whole force of the nation to check and nullify its pretensions and its power. We are glad, now that we see the facts with no veil of false pretense about them, to fight thus for the ultimate peace of the world and for the liberation of its peoples, the German peoples included: for the rights of nations great and small and the privilege of men everywhere to choose their way of life and of obedience. The world must be made safe for democracy. Its peace must be planted upon the tested foundations of political liberty. We have no selfish ends to serve. We desire no conquest, no dominion. We seek no indemnities for ourselves, no material compensation for the sacrifices we shall freely make. We are but one of the champions of the rights of mankind. We shall be satisfied when those rights have been made as secure as the faith and the freedom of nations can make them. . . .

It will be all the easier for us to conduct ourselves as belligerents in a high spirit of right and fairness because we act without **animus**,[2] not in **enmity**[3] towards a people or with the desire to bring any injury or disadvantage upon them, but only in armed opposition to an irresponsible government which has thrown aside all considerations of humanity and of right and is running amuck. We are, let me say again, the sincere friends of the German people, and shall desire nothing so much as the early reestablishment of intimate relations of mutual advantage between us,—however hard it may be for them, for the time being, to believe that this is spoken

---

[2] **animus**—feeling of animosity, ill will.

[3] **enmity**—hatred or ill will.

from our hearts. We have borne with their present Government through all these bitter months because of that friendship,—exercising a patience and forbearance which would otherwise have been impossible. We shall, happily, still have an opportunity to prove that friendship in our daily attitude and actions towards the millions of men and women of German birth and native sympathy who live amongst us and share our life, and we shall be proud to prove it towards all who are in fact loyal to their neighbors and to the Government in the hour of test. They are, most of them, as true and loyal Americans as if they had never known any other fealty of allegiance.[4] They will be prompt to stand with us in rebuking and restraining the few who may be of a different mind and purpose. If there should be disloyalty, it will be dealt with with a firm hand of stern repression; but, if it lifts its head at all, it will lift it only here and there and without **countenance**[5] except from a lawless and malignant few.

It is a distressing and oppressive duty, Gentlemen of the Congress, which I have performed in thus addressing you. There are, it may be, many months of fiery trial and sacrifice ahead of us. It is a fearful thing to lead this great peaceful people into war, into the most terrible and disastrous of all wars, civilization itself seeming to be in the balance. But the right is more precious than peace, and we shall fight for the things which we have always carried nearest our hearts,—for democracy, for the right of those who submit to authority to have a voice in their own Governments, for the rights and liberties of small nations, for a universal dominion of right by such a concert of free peoples as shall bring peace and safety to all nations and make the world itself at last free. To such a task we can dedicate our lives and our

---

[4] fealty of allegiance—loyalty of a citizen to his or her government.

[5] **countenance**—tolerance; approval.

fortunes, everything that we have, with the pride of those who know that the day has come when America is privileged to spend her blood and her might for the principles that gave her birth and happiness and the peace which she has treasured. God helping her, she can do no other.

QUESTIONS TO CONSIDER

1. Is Wilson reluctant or eager to declare war on Germany? How do you know?

2. What does Wilson mean when he says: "We have no selfish ends to serve. We desire no conquest, no dominion"?

3. Why do you suppose Wilson says more than once, "We have no quarrel with the German people"?

Over There with General Pershing

BY PETER I. BOSCO

America joined the war with enthusiasm. U.S. troops in France were led by General John Pershing who, by the end of the war, received the title General of the Armies of the United States. Only George Washington had previously held this title. The next excerpt introduces Pershing, describes the first engagements in which American troops were involved, and concludes with the lyrics George M. Cohan wrote in the popular song, "Over There."

The first American troops arrived in France on June 28, 1917. To the tired French people, exhausted by three years of **attrition**,[1] these fresh young men brought promise and new hope.

The "doughboys," the nickname (of disputed origin) of the American soldiers, had come to fight on the side of liberty. Many thought it repayment of the debt owed

---

[1] **attrition**—a gradual reduction of numbers or strength.

to France for having helped their forebears win the American Revolution.

On July 4, 1917, the city of Paris threw a hearty welcome for the doughboys. During the celebration, an American colonel named C.E. Stanton uttered four words that were to stir both the French and American nations: "Lafayette, we are here." (Stanton was referring, of course, to the French general who fought for the United States during the War of Independence.)

These first men were the nucleus of what would become a huge army called the American Expeditionary Force (AEF). General John "Black Jack" Pershing, of the Mexican expedition, was the man President Wilson chose to be commander-in-chief of the AEF.

Pershing was born in Missouri in 1860 into a family whose original, German name was Pfoersching. In 1886 he graduated from the United States Military Academy at West Point, top of his class. While serving in the U.S. Cavalry, he fought in the last Indian Wars of the American West.

In those days, promotions in rank were painfully slow. By his mid-thirties he was still a lieutenant. He considered leaving the Army to become a lawyer. His good friend Charles Dawes, future vice president of the United States (1925–29), convinced Pershing to stick with the Army a while longer. Neither of them could have dreamed that Pershing's Army career would sky-rocket him to international fame.

In 1898 Pershing fought in Cuba where he won the Silver Star. Next he went to the Philippines to help put down the Moro rebellion. Only a captain, Pershing won the admiration of President Theodore Roosevelt, who sent him to act as an observer in the Russo-Japanese War of 1904–05.

Roosevelt rewarded Pershing in 1906 by elevating him four ranks to brigadier general. Pershing, only 46 years old, had jumped over 862 senior officers, creating considerable bitterness among his fellow officers for many years.

Pershing's devotion to duty helped him to weather personal hardship. The day he arrived in Texas to lead the Mexican expedition, he received the news that his wife and three small daughters had burned to death in a fire at the Presidio Army base in San Francisco. Pershing went on with his mission and proved himself an able leader of men. When he returned, President Wilson made him a two-star general.

Wilson probably could not have made a better choice for commander of the AEF. Pershing was no great strategist and often lacked military wisdom. Yet, he had patience, emotional balance and unshakable fortitude—important qualities if one is to shape an army. Pershing's organization of the AEF from scratch was one of the great feats of World War I.

Pershing was the picture-perfect image of an **indomitable**[2] high commander. His height and rigid posture seemed tailor-made for monuments. He possessed a strength of character that inspired confidence in his men as well as his political superiors in Washington.

Most of all, Pershing had the grit and determination to stand up to the Allied governments and their generals. France and Britain were not interested in an independent and untested American Army. They needed men to bolster their thinned-out lines. They wanted to use American manpower to flesh out their depleted units.

Pershing said no. He was appalled by the callous disregard the Allied generals had for the lives of their troops. Casualties were just numbers to them. Pershing could not bear the thought of his men being dragged into some wasteful trench battle at the whim of foreign generals whom he considered to be incompetent strategists.

---

[2] **indomitable**—incapable of being overcome or subdued; unconquerable.

Not only was Pershing going to keep his Army intact and independent, he also intended to keep it away from the fighting until he felt it was fully trained. The Allies constantly pressured him to commit his troops, ready or not. They even put severe pressure on the American government to remove Pershing, but Wilson doggedly stuck by his general.

Pershing realized that the stateside training his men had received was inadequate for the kind of war that faced them at the front. New training areas were set up in the rear.

French troops, hardened veterans loaned to Pershing, became professors to the green Americans. The French instructors could hardly believe how ill-trained the doughboys were. Yet, in time, they were amazed by the speed and dedication with which these same Americans applied their new training and tactics.

In early October, Pershing arranged with General Pétain, commander-in-chief of the French army, to have small American units go into the French line for 10 days at a time for the sake of experience. Through this rotation system, most doughboys would be initiated into trench warfare.

The line around the city of Toul was the spot Pershing chose for the first rotations. This was one of the so-called "quiet sectors." Except for occasional shelling, sniping and trench raids, there had been no fighting there since 1914. Both sides seemed content to keep it that way.

Pershing chose this sector so his men could gain confidence without the risk of getting caught in a major attack and being mauled or beaten. A few weeks later the Germans discovered that the virgin American troops were now in the line. They decided to send a welcoming committee for the new arrivals.

At midnight on November 2, 1917, German infantrymen staged a well-executed raid on the American trench. After a short barrage, the Germans cut through the wire without being detected and infiltrated the American position. They did their bloody work and got away.

The Germans killed three doughboys and took 11 prisoners. Corporal Nick Mulhall had the unpleasant distinction of being the first U.S. soldier of the war to be captured. He was never seen or heard from again.

The raid was intended to humiliate the Americans and shake their morale. Far from it, the United States now had three heroes to rally around, and, the doughboys were eager to retaliate.

Thereafter, trench raids were frequent on both sides. On one occasion, Private Leslie Lane turned a corner and was confronted by a group of soldiers. Lane ducked down to get a better view of them against the dark night sky.

"I was asked in French if I would consent to become a prisoner," he recalled. "I thought it was one of our French friends fooling around . . . The questioner then asked me in quite fluent English."

Lane stepped forward to see that it was a German sergeant-major with a party of about 15 men. The big German grabbed Lane and tried to silence him. "I then kicked the fellow in a vulnerable spot so furiously," recalled Lane, "that it brought him to his knees."

Lane then shot the sergeant-major before he himself was knocked unconscious. The shot alerted the other Americans and the rest of the raiders scattered back to their line. Lane soon came to, only to feel the German sergeant-major quivering at his feet.

"I reached to get a hold of him so I could get up first, and in doing so, found that he had pulled the pin from a 'potato masher' grenade, which exploded as I grabbed his hand, shattering three fingers on my left hand."

Another soldier, who saw this, reported that Lane had been killed. As Lane struggled to crawl to a first aid station, an American sentry turned the corner.

"Knowing there were Germans around and thinking I was killed, he was taking no chances and made a lunge for me with his bayonet. I saw the gleam of the bayonet aimed at my throat and raised my injured hand to ward off the blow."

The bayonet mangled his hand even more. The sentry then realized it was Lane and apologized profusely. "But I had no time to listen," recalled Lane, "as I was bleeding to death and wanted to get to First Aid before it was too late."

The enthusiasm and vigor of the doughboys was refreshing to the tired Allied soldiers. The patriotic songwriter George M. Cohan put the spirit of the Americans to music. His most famous tune could be heard in every Allied trench, dugout and gunpit on the Western Front. French, British and American soldiers sang it while cleaning their guns. They whistled it while marching. They hummed it while they munched their hard biscuits and creamed beef.

Over there, over there,
Spread the word, send the word, over there,
That the Yanks are coming, the Yanks are coming,
The drums drum drumming everywhere.
So prepare, say a prayer.
Send the word, spread the word to beware,
We'll be over, we're coming over,
And we won't come back till it's over over there.

QUESTIONS TO CONSIDER

1. Why did the French ask that Pershing be removed as general shortly after he arrived in France?

2. According to Peter I. Bosco, what were the characteristics that made General Pershing such a fine leader?

3. What is the emotional impact of George M. Cohan's song, "Over There"?

At War on the Home Front

BY EDWARD F. DOLAN

The war effort was nationwide as people at home went to work making supplies needed for the war. Although there were some ugly moments, the war also meant opportunities.

No matter how divided they had been, once the United States entered the war, people at home quickly got to work providing the materials needed for the fighting. Crowding into factories all across the country, they began to produce everything from munitions to uniforms. Before the war ended, they had turned out, among other equipment, a half-million rifles, 3.5 billion bullets, and 20 million artillery shells.

One of the most important home-front tasks was to grow food, not only for the soldiers overseas and stateside but also for America's families and the people of the **beleaguered**[1] Allied nations. Thousands of men and women went to work on farms, increasing the nation's agricultural output by 25 percent. To make sure that the growing food supply was not wasted, the government urged the conservation of food. Everyone was asked to save leftovers for future meals. "Meatless Tuesdays" and "Porkless Thursdays" were introduced. Children were reminded to be "patriotic to the core" when eating apples and to waste nothing.

Another major task for those left at home was the construction of the ships needed to carry soldiers, equipment, and foodstuffs overseas. The government launched a huge shipbuilding program that eventually employed 350,000 workers in 341 shipyards. These workers produced hundreds of merchant vessels at a blinding rate of speed. On July 4, 1918, alone, ninety-five new ships were launched.

By 1918 the war was costing $44 million a day. To raise the needed money, the government increased taxes and embarked on a program of Liberty Loans. Under the loan program, Americans could purchase government bonds for a few dollars or, when children bought them, a few cents. The government promised to repay the loans at a later date and to add a profit in the form of interest. Liberty Loan campaigns brought in a total of more than $21 billion in sales.

Unfortunately, despite all the fine work and spirit going into the war effort, there was an ugly side to life on the home front. The nation's German Americans became the victims of a hate-inspired hysteria that gripped the United States immediately before the war and that lasted throughout it. This hysteria led to a variety of injustices. The teaching of the German language was banned in many high schools and universities. Eggs and garbage were thrown at some German American

---

[1] **beleaguered**—harassed, exhausted.

homes. Worst of all, a number (thankfully small) of innocent Germans were physically beaten, and one man was lynched by a drunken mob.

Some German Americans changed their names for safety's sake. Also changed were the names of things that had their origins in the German language. Hamburger steak and the German measles were rechristened "Liberty steak" and "Liberty measles." The dachshund dog was given the new name "Liberty pup."

Congress passed the Espionage Act of 1917 and the **Sedition**[2] Act of 1918, both aimed against possible spying and sabotage activities. Both were triggered in part by the anger of the times and in part by the valid worry that some German Americans (and others opposed to the war) might attempt to harm or slow the nation's home-front effort. About 1,900 cases were tried under the acts, although most of them came to nothing.

The hysteria was a waste of time and energy. The vast majority of German Americans were loyal citizens, and thousands of young German American men joined the armed forces and fought overseas.

AMERICAN WOMEN GO TO WAR

America's women were at work everywhere during World War I. They labored on the home front and overseas. They took jobs on the nation's farms, in factories, and in shipyards, and served in its military forces.

Approximately a million women filled the vacancies left by the men who were now in uniform. Many were young girls who had previously worked in local shops and department stores or who had never worked before. Many were wives who had once worked, but had left their jobs to raise families.

---

[2] **sedition**—conduct or language meant to incite rebellion against a government or authority.

Women on the farms were nicknamed "farmerettes" by the press. In the factories and shipyards, they served mainly as clerks, secretaries, typists, and bookkeepers.

World War I also marked an important "first" for American women. For the first time in the nation's history, women were permitted to join the armed forces. Some 13,000, known as "Yeomanettes," enlisted in the navy to do clerical work stateside. Nearly 300 entered the marine corps as clerks and won the name "Marinettes." More than 230 women traveled to France as part of the U.S. Army Signal Corps. There, they served as telephone operators for the American Expeditionary Force (AEF).

But they were not the only ones to travel overseas. Some 11,000 women, although not actual members of the armed forces, served abroad (as well as at home) as nurses; others became ambulance drivers. Women were also among the 6,000 Red Cross workers who sailed to France.

About 3,500 women served in the cafeterias and recreation facilities that the Young Men's Christian Association (YMCA) operated in England, France, and Russia. Members of the Young Women's Christian Association (YWCA) also provided services for women overseas and at home. More than fifty women of the Society of Friends (the Quakers) tended wounded soldiers on the western front and helped to feed and clothe civilians who lost their homes in the fighting.

Two groups of American women also served on the western front before the United States entered the war. One group was made up of the wives and daughters of American diplomats who were stationed in Europe at the time the fighting erupted in 1914. They tended to the needs of families left homeless by the fighting. The other was a unit of ambulance drivers—the American Ambulance in Paris—formed by women living in France.

Like the men of the AEF, the 25,000 American women who served overseas risked death, disease, and injury. An estimated 348 lost their lives. Some were killed in air raids and artillery bombardments. Others died or were left **debilitated**[3] by the diseases and disorders bred by the filthy and worse-than-primitive conditions along the western front.

The exact number of women who were injured is unknown. There are individual stories, however, that leave no doubt as to the seriousness of some of the injuries. When a hand grenade accidentally exploded near her, a writer and Red Cross worker sustained wounds that kept her hospitalized for two years. A woman doctor caught in a gas attack suffered burned lungs. A study conducted in the 1920s revealed that, among the women injured in the war, at least 200 were permanently disabled.

---

[3] **debilitated**—weakened.

QUESTIONS TO CONSIDER

1. How might a typical American family have shown its support for the war effort?

2. What was the "ugly side" to life on the home front?

3. U.S. entry into the war proved to be tremendously expensive. What are some of the ways the government raised the money to pay for war-related expenses?

4. How did the role of women in American society change as a result of World War I?

America at War

Leaving Ship The first American troops arrive in France, June 26, 1917.

James Montgomery Flagg, who became the "official artist" of New York State, stands by his famous image of Uncle Sam.

▼

Two of the recruitment posters
by Howard Chandler Christy.

◀ American marksmen hold this outpost in the Vosges with a French automatic rifle.

Field Artillery in the Argonne In the haze of early morning, at the edge of the tangle of stakes and wires that once marked No Man's Land, Americans pound the retreating German lines.
▼

▲

Soldiers of the 369th Regiment, U. S. Army march to the front.

Returning heroes They started out as New York's African American National Guard troop, but when the war was over American newspapers called them "Hell Fighters," and several were awarded the French Croix de Guerre for their heroism in the war. ▶

The Hello Girls To overcome the difficulties of the French telephone system, Pershing called for American women telephone operators. They were known as the "Hello Girls," and the press loved them. So did the troops they served. ▶

A traveling kitchen Women of the YWCA movement as well as from the Salvation Army joined troops in the field, where they distributed food under less-than-ideal circumstances. Their presence contributed much to morale. ▼

▲

Women in the Construction Industry As the men left to
fight in the war, women took on the jobs they left. Here rivet
heaters and passers take a break from work in the navy yard
at Puget Sound in Washington State to have their picture taken.

Hell Fighters

BY MICHAEL L. COOPER

This excerpt, from the book Hell Fighters: African American Soldiers in World War I, *tells the story of the 369th Regiment in France. The regiment began as a National Guard troop from Harlem in New York City. Before the war was over, several soldiers distinguished themselves, winning the French Croix de Guerre (War Cross) for their heroism.*

People of many races fought in the Great War. They included nearly a million black men from British and French colonies in Africa. Africans were among France's highest ranking army officers.

America, which had been supporting the Allies with vast shipments of food and ammunition, officially entered World War I on April 6, 1917, by declaring war on Germany. At that time, the United States had a very small army—only 130,000 men. By the end of the year, nearly four million men had either volunteered or been drafted into the army.

Some 400,000 of these soldiers were black. . . . Nearly 40,000 black soldiers became combat troops. They fought in France in the Ninety-second and Ninety-third Infantry Divisions. But the majority of black soldiers, because of their race, were assigned jobs as laborers at military bases in France and the United States.

The war was doubly difficult for these African Americans. They had to endure danger and hardships while burdened by their own country's racism. Black soldiers were just a small part of the Great War. Yet, while often overlooked, their bravery in battle and their work behind the front lines were significant contributions to their country's role in World War I.

The Fifteenth New York Voluntary Infantry Regiment was treated like an orphan for most of its short life. "The self-made regiment," said its commander, Colonel William Hayward, "started without traditions, without education, and without friends."

New York's African American National Guard troop was barely a year old in 1917 when the United States officially entered World War I. Few could have predicted that this hastily organized group of men would return from the European conflict as heroes.

The guardsmen learned the fundamentals of army life by meeting nights and weekends at a makeshift armory. It was not spacious like the white National Guard's brick-and-concrete armory downtown. The Harlem armory consisted of an old second-floor dance hall at 132nd Street and Seventh Avenue and, one block away, a former cigar store with a sign in the window that seemed to plead, "RECRUITS WANTED."

The first men to join the Fifteenth were given the rank of sergeant, although they knew as little about army life as the privates under their command. Few of the new guardsmen had proper uniforms. Some of them wore cartridge belts or bayonet scabbards.[1] And when the regiment marched along Harlem's streets, most of the men carried broomsticks instead of rifles.

Harlem residents regarded the Fifteenth New York with a mixture of curiosity and pride. The guardsmen wore civilian clothes and did not march very well, but they were the only African American National Guard regiment in the state and one of just six in the nation.

New York State's governor had created the Fifteenth a couple of years earlier at the urging of black leaders. He appointed a white lawyer, William Hayward, as the regiment's commander. Hayward, a forty-year-old friend of the governor's who had little military experience, was given the rank of colonel.

Colonel Hayward recruited other influential white men. Robert E. Lee's grandson, Dr. George Bolling Lee, was regimental physician. Hayward also persuaded young Hamilton Fish, whose family had been prominent in New York since the colonial era, to join by giving him the rank of captain. Fish's only previous experience leading men had been as the captain of the football team at Harvard University. Another officer was Arthur W. Little, who had been a magazine publisher in civilian life.

These men enlisted in the National Guard because they expected the United States to go to war in Europe. Most citizens did not want to get involved in a conflict that was so far away. Yet the war was going badly for America's traditional friends, France and Great Britain. A million German soldiers were entrenched in France. German submarines had blockaded the British Isles, cutting off shipments of food and other essential goods to the people.

Although officially a "colored" regiment, the Fifteenth was not completely black. The privates and

---

[1] scabbards—sheaths for holding weapons.

the noncommissioned officers, who were sergeants and corporals, were African American. Some commissioned officers—the lieutenants and captains—were of both races. The majors and the one colonel were all white.

The highest ranking black officer was Captain Napoleon Marshall, a Harvard graduate and a lawyer. Another black officer was Lieutenant Charles W. Fillmore. He was a veteran of the Spanish-American War and one of the businessmen who had urged the governor to create the regiment. A third officer was Lieutenant George B. Lacey. A former Chicago resident, Lacey had been a member of the Eighth Illinois, the nation's largest African American National Guard regiment.

The most famous officer of either color was Lieutenant James Reese Europe. This thirty-nine-year-old musician, known as "Big Jim," was a popular ragtime[2] band leader. After joining the Fifteenth, Lieutenant Europe recruited fifty musicians to form a regimental band. This band became one of the army's popular attractions.

Colonel Hayward knew a regimental band would help recruitment. He asked friends to donate money to buy instruments. John D. Rockefeller gave $1,000, and a tin can manufacturer gave $10,000. Europe searched the nightclubs of Manhattan, Chicago, and Puerto Rico for talented musicians willing to join the National Guard. One new recruit was the composer Noble Sissle. He was such a good musician he was given the rank of sergeant and soon promoted to lieutenant.

Big Jim's military band always played to large crowds, and, as Colonel Hayward predicted, it attracted recruits. "Hadn't been for that damn band," one soldier later complained, "I wouldn't be in the army."

The Fifteenth Regiment left Saint-Nazaire in early March. It traveled in small boxcars marked

---

[2] ragtime—music characterized by a strong syncopated rhythm.

"CHEVEAUX 8 HOMMES 40"[3] four hundred miles north to training camp near the battlefront, at Chalons [France]. The Harlem regiment was warmly welcomed.

"Our great American general put the black orphan in a basket, set it on the doorstep of the French, pulled the bell, and went away," one of the Fifteenth's officers told a French colonel wearing an "ENGLISH SPOKEN HERE" sign. And the colonel replied, "Welcome little black baby."

The French did not discriminate against black people as white Americans did. Over a half million blacks from France's African colonies had joined the French army. These colonials served at all ranks, including four colonels and two generals.

The New Yorkers had to adjust to new equipment and different customs. They thought French rifles were inferior to U.S. army rifles. The Americans also complained about the Gallic[4] habit of eating only soup and bread for dinner. But the men did enjoy one French custom—wine with meals.

The French customarily drink wine at lunch and dinner, so each day their soldiers received a canteen full of red wine. Instead of dividing it between the two meals, as the Frenchmen did, the Americans often drank theirs all at once. One doughboy[5] alarmed the whole camp when, after gulping the contents of his canteen, he began shooting at imaginary Germans. French commanders decided against giving the Americans wine; instead, they would receive a daily ration of sugar to use in their coffee.

The New Yorkers spent five weeks training. French instructors, assisted by translators, taught them about

---

[3] CHEVEAUX 8 HOMMES 40—French for "HORSES 8 MEN 40."

[4] Gallic—relating to France.

[5] doughboy—name for an American infantryman in World War I.

trench warfare, poison gas, and hand-to-hand combat. As they had been at Saint-Nazaire, the men were impatient to get to the fighting.

They constantly heard field cannons, which made deep rumbling noises like the sound of distant thunder, booming in the distance. A huge German attack was under way. "The boys keep looking at the big flashes in the north, and saying 'le's go,'" Major Little noted in his diary, "and we've formally adopted 'le's go' as the motto of this brunette fighting outfit."

AEF commanders gave the Fifteenth a new name, the 369th Regiment, U.S. Army, and in mid-April ordered it to the front. There the 369th would serve under General Henri Gouraud. The general had lost his right arm early in the war. He was a national hero. French soldiers, who called Gouraud the Lion of France, cheered whenever they saw him.

While marching to their positions at the front, the 369th came under fire for the first time. Artillery shells from German cannons eight to ten miles away whistled through the air and exploded nearby. The men's reaction surprised Major Little. They were "never really scared," he said, but "laughed and screamed in gleeful excitement."

As the Americans neared the front lines, they saw the awful devastation of war. Artillery barrages had reduced villages, which had been standing for hundreds of years, to rubble. The surrounding fields in previous springs would have been freshly plowed and sown with wheat. The countryside, one soldier said, had been "torn and horribly disfigured by shell burst or by pick and shovel." Instead of crops, there were thousands of little wooden crosses, each one marking a soldier's grave.

The 369th joined French soldiers at a camp only a few miles from the German army. The camp consisted of trenches and dugouts, which were underground shelters where the men slept. Some dugouts were furnished with beds, rugs, tables, chairs, and oil lamps looted from deserted homes. The trenches and the dugouts protected infantrymen from the flying shrapnel of exploding shells continuously fired by distant enemy artillery.

The French soldiers were glad to see the Americans. They had been fighting for three and one-half years. Many were **dispirited**.[6] Some had committed **mutiny**[7] the previous winter by refusing to go to the front. The Allies were worried that the French army would rebel against its generals. The doughboys' arrival gave the French new confidence and stopped the threat of rebellion.

Soldiers stationed near the front took turns at guard duty in the trenches on the edge of a narrow stretch of earth called no-man's-land. Where there had been a lot of fighting, no-man's-land was a forlorn area of mud, shell craters, splintered trees, and barbed wire. On the opposite side, only a few hundred feet away, German soldiers guarded their own trench row.

The Allies and Central Powers had been in a stalemate. The two enemies occupied similar lines of trenches nearly five hundred miles long. Each side had tried to overwhelm the other by sending hundreds of thousands of men into battle. But the armies were almost equally matched, and only a few miles of ground were ever won or lost.

The killing, on the other hand, was horrendous. Artillery and machine guns were used to slaughter huge numbers of men. The battle of the Somme, one of the war's worst battles, began in July of 1916. It lasted six months, and casualties on both sides exceeded one million men.

These big battles, though, were infrequent. Most of the time soldiers manned muddy or dusty trenches and

---

[6] **dispirited**—having low morale.

[7] **mutiny**—revolt against a superior officer.

waited for something to happen. Day-to-day life was miserable. The men complained the most about rain and rats. It rained so often soldiers developed trench foot, a numbing of the feet caused by standing for long periods in mud and water.

Thousands of rats boldly scurried about. They ate everything, from decomposing corpses to boots. Rats even gnawed through sleeping men's pants pockets searching for food.

The men also complained about cooties, or body lice, which infested every frontline soldier. On warm spring days, bare-chested men passed the time by "reading the shirt." They would hold their shirts up to the light as though reading a newspaper, but they were looking for lice.

Boredom became so unbearable that men sometimes took foolish chances for a little entertainment. One night, French soldiers heard a band playing on the German side. They crawled across no-man's-land and stopped beneath the barbed wire strung in front of the enemy's trenches to listen to the concert. The excursion ended when the Germans discovered their uninvited guests and tossed grenades over the wire.

Enemy fire and accidents killed or wounded someone every few days. Once, a soldier knocked a bag of grenades into a dugout where several members of the 369th were sleeping, and the explosion injured three men.

Raiding parties were another constant danger. Under the cover of darkness, enemy troops would sneak across to kill or capture Allied soldiers. The 369th had been on the front line for nearly a month when two of its men became heroes for repelling German raiders.

On the night of May 13, Privates Henry Johnson and Needham Roberts were on guard duty while three other men slept in a nearby dugout. Roberts heard the sound of wire cutters clipping barbed wire just a few yards away. As he yelled a warning to his sleeping comrades, a flare exploded overhead, signaling the raiders to attack.

The light from the flare revealed Germans, armed with pistols and knives, rushing through a gap in the barbed wire. The enemy soldiers lobbed grenades into the trenches, wounding both Americans. One explosion collapsed the front of the dugout, trapping the three men inside.

Roberts, though badly wounded, propped himself against the dugout door and threw a grenade at the approaching raiders. Johnson quickly fired all three shots from his rifle. Just after the last shot, a German soldier lunged at him. The American used his rifle as a club and splintered the wooden stock across his attacker's head.

Johnson saw two enemy soldiers picking up Roberts to carry him away as a prisoner. He leaped on one German's back and plunged his nine-inch bolo knife into the top of the man's head.

By then, the man Johnson had knocked down with his rifle was on his feet, shooting at the American. A bullet hit the doughboy's side, and he sank to his knees. The attacker rushed over to finish off the fallen man. As the grim-faced German hesitated over the doughboy, Johnson summoned all of his strength and lunged upward, thrusting his already bloody knife into the man's gut. The other raiders, hearing the sound of approaching soldiers, fled back across no-man's-land.

The French government awarded both Johnson and Roberts the Croix de Guerre, a medal bestowed for heroism and **gallantry**.[8] Reporters interviewed the two men in their hospital beds. Stories about the fight appeared in many U.S. newspapers and magazines. Because the war's horrible battles were frequently described as

---

[8] **gallantry**—spirited bravery.

hells, and the enemy described as devils, African American newspapers began calling the 369th Hell Fighters. It was a nickname the Harlem regiment proudly accepted. "Our colored volunteers from Harlem," Major Little observed, "had become in a day one of the famous fighting regiments of the World War." Henry Johnson and Needham Roberts were the first men in the 369th Regiment to win medals for bravery, but not the last.

QUESTIONS TO CONSIDER

1. How did the French and the Americans differ in their treatment of black soldiers?

2. Why do you think 400,000 African Americans enlisted in spite of discrimination at home and in the army?

3. Why were the soldiers of the 369th Regiment called the "Hell Fighters"?

Three Heroes

BY DON LAWSON

Among the airmen and soldiers of the American Expeditionary Force (AEF), there were exceptional people. Eddie Rickenbacker was America's answer to the Red Baron. A true leader as well as an ace fighter pilot, he led his Hat-in-the-Ring squadron to score the highest number of Allied aerial victories. One of his pilots, Frank Luke, is an example of how wartime can make heroes of people who might not fit into a peacetime world. And Corporal Alvin York, later Sergeant York, used the skills he learned hunting in the hills of Tennessee to capture 132 German soldiers all by himself!

EDDIE RICKENBACKER

Eddie Rickenbacker was the kind of war hero that Americans on both the home front and fighting front took to their hearts. He was a young man who had come up the hard way, but he had learned something with each step along that difficult path.

Born in Columbus, Ohio, in 1890, he was one of seven children whose father died when Eddie was twelve years of age.

The day after Eddie's father was buried, the youngster went to work in a local factory, earning $3.50 a week. He worked the night shift, walking to and from the factory to save carfare. At the end of each week he turned over his entire pay to his mother. This love for his mother was to give Eddie Rickenbacker strength all of his life, even when he grew up and became America's top fighter pilot. On one of his most difficult days in the air war against Germany, the fabric ripped from one of the wings of his Nieuport pursuit ship, and it looked as if he were going to crash and be killed. He thought of what a tragic blow the news of his death would be to his mother, and the picture of her grief gave him the renewed courage and determination that enabled him to bring his battered plane back across the Allied lines.

As a boy still in his teens young Eddie became interested in motors, and he took correspondence courses in engineering and drafting. When he was 20 he took up automobile racing and was soon winning championships in the United States and abroad. He was in England when America entered World War I. He had hurried home eager to suggest his plan for a squadron of flyers composed of racing-car drivers. When that plan had been turned down, Rickenbacker had gladly accepted General Pershing's offer to accompany him to France—mainly because he wanted to be near the front. As Pershing had anticipated, Rickenbacker had not been in France very long before he asked for a transfer to the Air Service.

He was sent to Tours in France for his first flight training in August 1917. His natural mechanical ability plus a supreme desire to become a combat flyer made it possible for Rickenbacker to take his first solo flight after only 12 trips with an instructor. After only a few more hours of training (in World War II a fighter pilot had several hundred hours of flight training before he was sent into combat), Rickenbacker was transferred to the 94th Aero Pursuit Squadron.

The planes of the 94th bore a red-white-and-blue insignia. This design included an Uncle Sam stovepipe hat with stars and stripes on its crown. The hat was encircled by a ring, giving the unit its nickname: the Hat-in-the-Ring squadron. It was to become the most famous of all the American pursuit squadrons.

The Hat-in-the-Ring squadron was the first American-trained air unit to go into action against the enemy. It served longer in combat than any other air service squadron. It was credited with shooting down the first and last German airplanes shot down by the American Air Service. It shot down 69 planes, more than any other American squadron. It had the first official American Ace, Lieutenant Douglas Campbell, as well as the greatest American Ace, Captain Eddie Rickenbacker.

When Rickenbacker reported for duty with the Hat-in-the-Ring squadron, it was commanded by Major Raoul Lufbery, a veteran flyer who had shot down 17 planes while flying with the Lafayette Escadrille before America entered the war. . . .

Lufbery was not merely famous because of his individual combat record. He was also highly regarded as a leader. As commander of the Escadrille he worked out a number of aerial tactics to use against Germany's leading Ace, Baron Manfred von Richthofen, and his Flying Circus. Richthofen's red-nosed Fokkers were the **scourge**[1] of the air over the Western Front, particularly when they adopted mass formation flying against the Allied airmen.

Against these mass attacks Lufbery had his men form their planes into a circle in the air with each plane protecting the plane in front. When the men of the Lafayette Escadrille were flying two-place ships with an observer in the rear, the observer could pick off any

---

[1] **scourge**—source of punishment or affliction.

German plane that tried to enter this circle. This maneuver was based on the method American pioneers used in drawing their covered wagons into a circle in protection against the Indians. This "Lufbery Show" or "Lufbery Circle" was used by all air forces in fighter-plane combat right up through the Korean War.

Before his death Major Lufbery was able to take Eddie Rickenbacker and Douglas Campbell on their first flight over the German lines. Lufbery's careful instruction and the watchful way in which he shepherded his inexperienced flyers in their first flights were lessons Rickenbacker never forgot. When he himself was placed in command of the Hat-in-the-Ring squadron in September 1918, Rickenbacker was like a watchful father over his untried young flyers. Not only did he lead them on their first patrols as Lufbery had done, but on more than one occasion Rickenbacker credited them with victories that he could truly have claimed for himself. Rickenbacker finally was credited with 26 victories, but every member of his command agreed that he shot down at least a dozen other planes for which he received no credit.

Rickenbacker's sense of fair play went even further. Today, when **chivalry**[2] in warfare seems perhaps dead, a line from the diary of America's greatest air hero of World War I still has a gallant ring. On March 10, 1918, Rickenbacker wrote: "I will never shoot a Hun[3] who is at a disadvantage, regardless of what he would do in such a position."

Rickenbacker's personal code in leading his own men into battle was also a noble one. He never asked one of his pilots to fly a combat patrol he himself would not fly. In addition he made it a point of honor never to let a member of his squadron fly more hours against the

---

[2] **chivalry**—conduct characterized by honor.

[3] Hun—derogatory name for a German, especially a German soldier.

enemy than their leader. More than once Rickenbacker went on voluntary patrols when the day's regular patrols had been flown just to make certain he was taking his equal share of risk.

The Hat-in-the-Ring squadron first flew into combat from Toul in April 1918. On April 14 Lieutenant Alan Winslow and Lieutenant Douglas Campbell shot down the squadron's first planes. Within a month Rickenbacker was an Ace.

During their first weeks in combat the 94th flew French Nieuports. These were not the best planes in the air, by any means. There were no American planes available, however, and the American squadrons had to do the best they could with the planes they received from the Allies. Later the Hat-in-the-Ring squadron, as well as the 95th Aero Pursuit Squadron with whom the 94th shared an airfield, flew French Spads. The Spad was more of a match for the German Fokker, although the Fokker could fly higher and dive more swiftly than the Spad. The best of the British ships at this period of the war was the Sopwith Camel. During the entire war Camel pilots shot down more than 1,600 aircraft, more than fighter pilots flying any other type of plane have ever shot down.

In May the American Air Service had four squadrons at the front—the 27th, 94th, 95th, and 147th. These squadrons were formed into the 1st Pursuit Group. In July the 1st Pursuit Group played a key role during the Second Battle of the Marne as they fought the famed Richthofen Flying Circus to a standstill. It was during this fighting that young Quentin Roosevelt was killed.

Baron von Richthofen was now dead, and his Circus was commanded by a Captain Wilhelm Reinhardt. Later the Richthofen Circus was led by Hermann Goering, who scored 22 victories in World War I. This was the same Goering who would one day become the head of

Germany's *Luftwaffe*[4] during World War II. During the month they faced each other in daily combat during the Second Battle of the Marne, the 1st Pursuit Group suffered 36 pilot casualties and the Richthofen Circus had 38 men shot down.

The record of victories of the American Air Service grew as its pilots learned new lessons in daily combat against the enemy. Eddie Rickenbacker was an especially determined student. He was not a wild, reckless flyer, nor a lone wolf. He was a team flyer in every sense of the word. Although brave and daring, he did not believe in flying into battle in a blind rage and thus putting himself at a disadvantage against a more coldly calculating enemy. Just as he had done all of his life up to now, he set out to learn the "why" and "how" of his job. It was a matter of life and death that he do so. Aerial warfare was a grim, unforgiving business. Few pilots survived even one mistake. Evidence of this was the fact that during the course of the war the 94th Pursuit squadron suffered a 100 per cent turnover in flying personnel because of dead or wounded pilots.

Rickenbacker soon learned that a successful pursuit pilot had to know the limitations of his own aircraft. If the wings on a Nieuport buckled in pulling out of a fast dive, then it was up to the wise Nieuport pilot not to try and outdive a Fokker. If a Spad had certain other limitations against a Fokker, then it was up to the Spad pilot to recognize those limitations. Another observation he was forced into making was that all too often when he had an enemy in his gunsights, his guns would suddenly jam. He decided that irregularities in some shell casings caused the jamming. To avoid this he personally inspected every shell that was placed in the machine-gun belts of his aerial guns. He instructed the men who flew with him to do likewise.

---

[4] *Luftwaffe*—the German air force.

Slowly but surely these knowledgeable actions began to pay off and Rickenbacker's personal victory tally began to mount. He was awarded a number of French and American decorations, including the highest award given its military men by the United States: the Congressional Medal of Honor. He received the Medal of Honor for fearlessly attacking seven enemy planes and shooting down two of them while he was flying a voluntary patrol.

As a team flyer, however, Rickenbacker was not satisfied with only his personal achievement. He wanted his team, the Hat-in-the-Ring squadron, to lead all other American squadrons. When he assumed command of the 94th, the 27th squadron had a larger total number of victories. Rickenbacker told all of the Hat-in-the-Ring mechanics that he wanted every pursuit ship in the squadron ready for flight duty every day. He told his pilots that he expected the 94th to gain the lead in victories within a few days and never lose it. Rather than spur his men on by getting them to compete among themselves, he urged the 94th to compete as a team against all of the other squadrons of the American Air Service.

Rickenbacker assumed command of the 94th squadron on September 15 at the peak of the St. Mihiel offensive. On his first day in combat after being named the Hat-in-the-Ring squadron commander Rickenbacker shot down two German planes just to fulfill his part of the challenge he had just given his men. Fired by the follow-me spirit of their leader, the flyers of the 94th Hat-in-the-Ring squadron soon took over the lead in aerial victories and held it until the end of the war.

FRANK LUKE

Not all flyers, however, were able to adopt Rickenbacker's wise, sane, team-play approach to aerial combat. There were others who flew with reckless gallantry into battle and scored spectacular victories day-after-incredible-day—men who lived alone, fought alone, and all too frequently died alone. It was because of the feats of one such man that the 27th Aero Squadron temporarily led the 94th Aero Squadron in total victories. This heroic lone wolf was Frank Luke, the balloon buster from Arizona. . . .

During a period beginning on September 12, the first day of the St. Mihiel campaign, and ending just 17 days later, Frank Luke shot down 18 or 19 enemy balloons and airplanes. This was more aircraft than any other member of the American Air Service had shot down at this time. His career as a pursuit pilot ended with his death in a church graveyard at Murvaux, France, on September 29. He died at the age of 21.

Born at Phoenix, Arizona, in 1897, Frank Luke was one of nine children. Their father was a German immigrant. Young Frank went to work in a local copper mine after graduating from high school. He was uncommunicative and had few friends. When America went to war, one of Frank's brothers enlisted in the Army and his sister Eva became a Red Cross nurse. It was Eva who talked Frank into joining the Signal Corps. He wasn't interested in the infantry because he disliked discipline of any kind, but he thought that as a member of the Signal Corps he could get to be a pursuit pilot and continue to lead an independent life of action.

After preliminary flight training in the United States Frank was commissioned a second lieutenant on January 23, 1918. He was then sent to France, where he took advanced flight training at Issoudun, learning to fly Nieuports and Spads. He was assigned to the 27th Aero Pursuit Squadron of the 1st Pursuit Group near Château-Thierry in late July 1918. Later the squadron was moved to Rembercourt near Verdun.

On one of his very first flights over the enemy lines Frank was carefully instructed by his squadron commander to stay in formation. Luke decided, however, to go Hun-hunting on his own. When asked afterward why he had dropped out of formation, Luke said he had engine trouble. A day or two later he returned from one of these lone-wolf flights insisting he had shot down a German Fokker, but no one would believe him. After that he carried a pad of paper and a pencil with him. Whenever he shot down a German plane or balloon he landed at the nearest Allied position and got front-line observers to confirm his claim.

His flying companion—Luke continued to have few friends—came to be Lieutenant Joseph Wehner. Wehner's ancestry, like Luke's, was German, and Luke felt this gave them a common bond.

Luke had not flown in combat long before he became interested in the possibility of shooting down enemy observation balloons. Most Allied fighter pilots shied away from attacking German balloons because they were heavily defended by anti-aircraft guns as well as by several squadrons of fighter planes. This, plus the fact that it was rumored that each German balloon cost about $100,000, was a challenge that Luke could not resist.

On September 12 Luke went into action and shot down his first Drachen, as the German balloons were called. A few days later he shot down several more. By this time he and Wehner had worked out a system for Luke's attacks. While the Arizona balloon buster was roaring in to attack the balloons, Wehner flew nearby to protect him from German Fokkers. The two pursuit pilots also discovered that the best time to attack the balloons was right at dusk when the Drachen were being lowered to the ground.

On September 16 Luke and Wehner collaborated to shoot down another trio of balloons. Word had been going up and down the front about the 27th Aero Squadron's mounting victories, and Colonel Billy

Mitchell was on hand to watch Luke and Wehner put on their show on this evening. He saw each one of the three balloons go up in flames, and when Luke and Wehner returned to the field Mitchell counted over 100 bullet holes in the two men's airplanes. Their ships were repaired by the following day, however, and they went out and scored additional victories.

On September 18 Luke put on what was perhaps his greatest show when he bagged two more balloons, two Fokkers, and an observation plane. To set one of the balloons on fire, he had to fly within 50 feet of the ground. Finishing off the second balloon, he saw that Joe Wehner was in trouble, and he dived into a squadron of Fokkers, shooting down two of them. He then high-tailed it for home but managed to bag an observation ship before reaching his field. His tally was now three or four planes (the records vary) and ten balloons, giving him 13 or 14 victories to Eddie Rickenbacker's nine. But this proved to be a joyless day for Luke. Joe Wehner failed to return from this mission.

Luke had never spoken more than a few single-syllable words to his fellow flyers. Now he refused to talk to anyone, and he seemed to think of nothing but getting back into combat. Bad weather, however, prevented him from taking to the air until September 26. That day he shot down a Fokker, and the next day he bagged a balloon. To knock down this balloon, he had to come down to within 25 or 30 feet of the ground and fly through a flaming wall of defensive fire.

On September 29, his last day in the air, Luke spotted three enemy balloons near Verdun. Following his custom of making certain that he got credit for his victories, Luke dropped a message to some Allied front-line observers telling them to keep their eyes on the trio of *Drachen*. Within a matter of minutes he had set the first one aflame. On this attack, however, he was jumped by nine or ten Fokkers and was badly wounded.

Ignoring the wound and the fact that his Spad was also seriously damaged, he roared in to knock down the second balloon. The Fokkers kept after him, causing further damage to his ship. As he flew in to get the third balloon, he was faced with an inferno of anti-aircraft fire, but he flew unwaveringly through it and scored his final victory. In an apparent effort to avoid the Fokkers who lay in wait for him, Luke took evasive action and headed toward the Meuse River flying at treetop level.

As he approached the village of Murvaux he saw that its streets were filled with German troops. He machine-gunned them before his plane was forced down in the local church graveyard. As soon as he landed, Luke whipped out his automatic and managed to struggle from his plane. In a few moments he was completely surrounded by German infantry who demanded that he surrender. Luke's response was to empty his automatic at them. The Germans opened up with point-blank rifle fire, and moments later the balloon buster from Arizona lay dead.

For conspicuous gallantry on his last flight, Lieutenant Frank Luke was **posthumously**[5] awarded the Congressional Medal of Honor. Many years later Luke Air Force Base in Arizona was named for him.

CORPORAL (later SERGEANT) YORK

"Well, Corporal," Brigadier General Lindsay said, "I understand we don't have to do any more fighting."

"How's that, sir?" the corporal asked.

General Lindsay grinned. "Because your company commander tells me you just captured the whole blasted Hun army."

---

[5] **posthumously**—after death.

Corporal Alvin York looked uncomfortable. "I guess it wasn't quite the whole army, sir. Just a hundred and thirty-two of 'em."

"Just a hundred and thirty-two!"

"Yes, sir."

The General exploded with laughter. "Single-handed?" he managed to ask.

"More or less, sir."

General Lindsay shook his head with amazement.

Men all along the Western Front were equally amazed when they learned about York's feat. They just could not believe that one man could capture that many German infantrymen—and crack Prussian Guards at that. But the story was true, every word of it.

Corporal Alvin York—who later became world-famous as Sergeant York—was a mountain man from Fentress County, Tennessee. He had not wanted to join the Army. He had, in fact, been a conscientious objector[6] because of his religious beliefs. His pastor, however, as well as his first commanding officer in the Army had persuaded him that it was his moral duty to serve his country in this war. Once convinced that America and the Allies were fighting for the right, York became a soldier—and a great one.

York was a member of the 82nd Division. Men from Georgia, Alabama, and Tennessee were the backbone of this hard-fighting outfit, but a number of its members also came from many of the other states of the Union. For this reason the 82nd was often called the All-American Division.

Corporal York's heroic deed in the Argonne was performed on October 8, the day after the Lost Battalion was relieved. On this day York and 15 other men of the 82nd Division's 328th Infantry Regiment were led by

---

[6] conscientious objector—one who refuses to participate in military service or bear arms on the grounds of specific principles.

Sergeant Bernard Early in an attack on a German machine-gun battalion.

By crawling forward . . . the 16 men managed to work their way to the rear of the machine-gun nests. They then rushed one of the positions, capturing several officers and men. Other Germans only 40 or 50 yards away saw this action and turned their guns on the Americans. Before the Germans fired, however, they called to their comrades who had been taken prisoner, telling them to fall to the ground. Then the German machine gunners raked the American infantrymen, killing six of them and wounding three. Sergeant Early was one of the men who was wounded.

York now took command. He placed the German prisoners in the hands of the unwounded Americans. Then he worked out a plan to defeat the remaining Germans single-handed. His plan was based on his many years of experience in turkey-shooting contests back in Tennessee. In a turkey shoot a bird would be tied behind a log so that only its head could bob up occasionally. The marksman had to shoot and hit the turkey's head in the brief instant it was visible above the log. York now brought his ability as a turkey-shooting marksman into play. In order to try and draw a bead on York the Germans had to raise their heads above the sandbags that protected their machine-gun nests. Whenever a German raised his head, York picked him off.

After York had killed about a dozen of the Germans, a Prussian officer and half a dozen men charged him. Once again the Tennessee mountain man called upon his experience as a hunter. Rather than shoot the German nearest to him, York first picked off the last man, then the next-to-last and so on. Afterwards he explained that this was how wild turkeys were shot, so that the ones in front didn't know the ones in back were being hit. In this fashion York dropped all of the onrushing attackers before any of them knew what was happening to the others.

The German major in charge of the Prussian Guard machine-gun battalion now offered to surrender his command of about 90 men—if York would please just stop shooting. York signalled the Germans to come forward with their hands in the air. As they filed toward him, York saw that one of the Germans was carrying a half-concealed hand grenade. York shot him, and the rest of the prisoners fell meekly into line. York placed the major in front of him and told the other Americans to bring up the rear with the remaining prisoners.

The German major tried to point out the path they should follow, but York led his party in the opposite direction. He knew the major was trying to lead him into a trap.

As they moved toward the American lines they encountered more and more German machine-gun nests. With York prodding him in the back with his service revolver, the major urged his fellow soldiers to cry, "Kamerad!," which was the word the Germans used when they wanted to surrender.

York disarmed these new prisoners and added them to his bag for the day. Finally they reached the American lines, and he reported to his company commander, Lieutenant Ralph Woods, telling him he had a few Germans to turn over to him.

"How many are there, Corporal?" Lieutenant Woods asked.

"I kind of lost track, sir."

In addition to the 132 prisoners he had captured, the Tennessee corporal who had never wanted to be a soldier had killed some 20 Germans and silenced about 40 machine guns.

QUESTIONS TO CONSIDER

1. Which of the three heroes do you admire most? Why?

2. How did the backgrounds and personalities of Rickenbacker, Luke, and York influence their approach to combat?

3. Drawing on the experiences of these three heroes, why do you think teamwork is so vital on the battlefield?

The Woman
Physician

BY LETTIE GAVIN

Women served in the First World War in a number of ways. The armed forces accepted women into non-combat roles, supporting troops as nurses, cooks, and administrative assistants. Service organizations, such as the Red Cross, the Salvation Army, and the YMCA, sent women members to Europe to help the troops. But the era was one in which professional women, such as doctors, were few and had a tough time being taken seriously.

Dr. Mary Merritt Crawford was a female physician who had to forge her own path to service in World War I. Dr. Crawford attracted attention in 1908 as the first female ambulance surgeon at Williamsburg Hospital in Brooklyn, NY. A graduate of Cornell Medical School, she had been hired by Williamsburg because she scored higher than the male applicants in a competitive examination for internships. A crowd always gathered to see her hop aboard the rickety horse-drawn ambulance, she recalled. "I was a sensation," she said. "But you see, there wasn't much going on in the world in those days."

Dr. Crawford had risen to the post of chief surgeon at Williamsburg and had set up a private practice in Brooklyn when war loomed overseas in 1914. She decided to go to France.

> I wrote to three or four places and applied, and wrote to Dr. [Joseph] Blake of the American Ambulance Hospital [near Paris], but to no avail. Then one day my mother saw a newspaper notice that the Countess of Talleyrand, who was [the U.S. heiress] Anna Gould, had sent a thousand dollars to the "New York Sun" to pay the fare of American doctors to come to France. Military doctors were badly needed.
>
> She had asked Dr. Rambeau, who was head of the Pasteur Institute in New York, to select the doctors. I went right over [to see him], and he passed me. The "Sun" gave me a ticket on the old [ship] Rochambeau. They gave me a ticket to return . . . and twenty dollars in gold. Ten dollars to get me from Havre to Paris, and ten dollars to get me from Paris back to Havre. (Also told me not to expect anything more from them.)

Dr. Crawford sailed for France in September 1914, shortly after the war began. She reached Paris after a slow trip, only to be told by Madame Talleyrand that the French didn't need any doctors. "She didn't have anything for me," Dr. Crawford recalled. "I was pretty well flattened, you know, because I'd come over there and I didn't have much money, though I had my ticket home. But I wasn't going to go home. I stayed at the Ambulance [Hospital] until I could see what to do. I wrote letters to all the doctors on the staff and waited. I almost signed up to go down to Barcelona and take care of the typhoid epidemic which was going on there, because I was NOT going to go home."

But Dr. Crawford was finally introduced to the famed U.S. surgeon Joseph Blake by his secretary at the hospital. Dr. Crawford asked if she could witness his operations that day and followed him into the surgery. However, the anesthetist wasn't there. Dr. Blake looked around, furious. He was a big man and not used to being kept waiting by interns and young doctors. He turned to Dr. Crawford and barked, "Can you give ether?"

Dr. Crawford could and did. "I gave four anesthetics, one right after the other for him that morning. I was just in heaven. That afternoon the medical board was meeting and they had intended to turn me down [but] Blake said that he had taken me on as an anesthetist. Then Dr. DuBouchet, who was the other chief, said he'd take me on as anesthetist in the afternoon. So by nightfall, I had a full-time job." Later, she asked Dr. Blake to put her in charge of detail work for a ward of twenty to forty men. "He gave me a ward, then two, and finally I wound up with four wards, doing the dressings, taking the history of them, and looking after them. I tell you I worked hard."

Unfortunately, she did not do a great deal of surgery, largely due to Dr. Blake's **mercurial**[1] temperament. One week he told her, "I wish to heaven you could teach these young fellows to work the way you work and do the things that you do." The next week he placed a new male arrival from New York ahead of her. "I, suddenly, having been perfectly independent, found

---

[1] **mercurial**—quick and changeable in temperament; volatile.

myself being ordered around by this young doctor. . . . I wouldn't take it." When she confronted Dr. Blake about it, he said, "I'll never put a woman over a man," to which she replied, "What kind of a service have you got then?"

Meanwhile, the French had offered Dr. Crawford a job heading up their half of the hospital. Originally, she had refused, not wanting to lose the opportunity to train with Dr. Blake, but after her conversation with him, she accepted the French offer. "They put me on and I finished up with them," she recalled. She was somewhat disappointed in her new position, however. The French doctor she worked with was "very fussy and thought he must do everything [himself]. . . . I assisted him and that's all. When he found out I was leaving, he did allow me to amputate a couple of legs."

In treating her patients, Dr. Crawford remembered that

> We used a lot of things that nobody uses now. One interesting fact about that service: I saw the beginning of inventions. Giving a man a bath— we had a framework over an ordinary tub with extensions for his arms and legs. We could wash him and pour water on him, but we could keep water away from a part that shouldn't be touched. Dr. [Alexis] Carrel who was over there at Juilly came down and showed us his Carrel solution—irrigating the wound—and I saw the beginning of that. All sorts of contraptions were invented. That's one thing about medicine. A war benefits medicine more than it benefits anybody else. It's terrible, of course, but it does.

QUESTIONS TO CONSIDER

1. Judging from what she has said, what was Dr. Crawford's chief difficulty during the war?

2. Why do you suppose Crawford was so determined to stay in France?

3. What is ironic about Crawford's suggestion that "a war benefits medicine more than it benefits anybody else"?

Entertaining the Troops

**BY JAMES W. EVANS AND
GARDNER L. HARDING**

**ILLUSTRATIONS BY NEYSA McMEIN, ANITA
PARKHURST, AND ETHEL RUNDQUIST**

*As in other wars of the twentieth century, entertainers—singers,
actors, musicians—traveled to the front to provide
some moments of pleasure to soldiers during their
allotted rest periods. For the women in such
groups, the job went beyond performing on
stage and included social activities, such
as dancing. The following illustrations,
collected and published in 1921, give a
lighthearted picture of their work.*

"This is that famous scene 'over there.'
Arriving in a strange town, preferably late at
night, and finding nary a 'Y' representative
or an army man to meet us."

"The sore-throated and wet-footed soprano, ruining her voice for the sake of her country, while the young gallant shields her with his marvelous find—yes, an umbrella."

"To come back from the front for the three-day rest and see a regular girl again—one who could 'parlez Americaine'—was the height of many an ambition."

"'Sleeping cars! Insomnia!' Words not in the entertainer's vocabulary. After a few months, one could travel atop a supply truck and sleep as soundly as in one's own trundle bed."

"The Performance de Luxe. Aided by a pin or two, a much-appreciated dishpan 'mirror,' and a lot of chatter, one can (even in a six-by-ten room) make oneself a wondrous sight for the boys who have seen naught but uniforms for many a month."

"Dancing is generally conceded to be a pleasure, but when one has, in the space of a few months, danced 78,571 miles—or three times the distance around the earth—it ceases to be such. With smiling faces and aching limbs, in heavy shoes and hot uniforms, before breakfast, through lunch hours, on stone, on wood, on cinder floors, or on no floors at all, they danced."

QUESTIONS TO CONSIDER

1. What were the benefits and the drawbacks of being sent to entertain the troops during World War I?

2. What do you think was the most important job these entertainers had?

The Hello Girls

BY DOROTHY AND CARL J. SCHNEIDER

Affectionately known as "Hello Girls," the telephone switchboard operators of the U.S. Army Signal Corps supported communications among Pershing's troops and with other Allied forces in France. The authors of this excerpt write, "They caught the public's imagination. They were widely praised for their courage, dedication to duty, and efficiency, as glowing examples of American womanhood at its finest, rising to the emergency, standing shoulder to shoulder with their brothers-in-arms.... Journalists wrote story after story about them; servicemen stood in line to dance with them; an Army unit sent them horses to ride; generals commended and decorated them; and civilians and military alike waxed lyrical about them."

In the spring of 1918 a small group of women each dressed in what the Army Signal Corps described as chic blue serge suits and fashionable wide-brimmed hats posed for a picture on the roof of the AT&T building in New York City. They were proudly wearing a uniform prescribed by the Army for the Woman's Telephone Unit and adorned with U.S. Army Signal

Corps insignia and badges of rank and function. These thirty-three bilingual women sailed for Europe early in March 1918 aboard the troop ship *Celtic*; from Southampton a channel steamer transported them to France, where they took up their duties of running army telephone switchboards for the American Expeditionary Force, and coping with the operators of the French telephone system, who rarely spoke English. Before the Armistice five more units of American operators followed the first, bringing their numbers to 233.

General Pershing himself had fought the War Department to get them there. Initially, some of his staff had opposed bringing American women to France to serve so closely with army troops. But necessity overcame male reluctance. With the United States ill-prepared to fight, General Pershing's problems were **exacerbated**[1] by the **vagaries**[2] of a telephone system where the operators spoke a foreign language and seemed to have adopted the infamous **obstructionism**[3] of French bureaucrats. Two-hour delays and abrupt cut-offs roused American denunciations of French operators that rivaled attacks on the Hun. Every long-distance call required the cooperation of telephone exchanges in all the cities and towns along the line, a process complicated, muttered General Harbord, by "all the delays that could be born of French curiosity, conservatism and **cupidity**."[4] Misunderstandings pyramided. The United States Army needed telephone operators who could also interpret, often on matters of vital importance where a misconstrued message could spell disaster. Bilingual operators were particularly crucial in the early days

[1] **exacerbated**—made worse or more severe, aggravated.
[2] **vagaries**—erratic, unreliable actions.
[3] **obstructionism**—deliberate interference with progress.
[4] **cupidity**—greed.

before the Signal Corps could string its own lines and install its own equipment; but afterwards also reliable communication with the French military had to be maintained.

Even in the unlikely event that the Signal Corps could muster enough trained bilingual soldiers to provide good service, was this the most efficient use of its manpower? The British had already employed women behind the lines, releasing male troops for more dangerous duties. So when the correspondent Rheta Childe Dorr told General Pershing of her distress at seeing American "men in uniform working at card indexes, sorting mail, pounding typewriters and attending the telephone," Pershing assured her that "we shall have to have women telephone operators."

It probably helped that Americans expected to hear a pleasant woman's voice—widely advertised as the "Voice with the Smile" when they picked up a phone. The morale-building effect of their presence upon nostalgic American officers and troops may not have inspired General Pershing's request for the women telephone operators, but it provided a fringe benefit. "It broke up the blues," wrote a war correspondent. "I wanted to give three cheers. . . . I breathed a silent prayer that all the hello girls in the world might prosper and marry well. I reckon that the well-modulated, courteous and very American accents of a hello girl dripping in at the left ear have much the same effect on a homesick American as the soothing hand of a nurse on a sick soldier."

The War Department assigned responsibility for selecting and training the operators to the American Telephone and Telegraph Company. Ma Bell sought recruits among her own daughters, but could not find enough bilingual operators. The first call to the public for French-speaking volunteers went out on November 13, 1917—and evoked 7,000 responses. Eliminating women insufficiently fluent in French, women with male relatives overseas, and women with German connections, AT&T chose from the many fully qualified women the hundred Pershing had requested for the first contingent.

All the women selected for the first several units spoke fluent French, but most had little or no telephone experience. At camp switchboards and in toll offices at seven training centers, AT&T provided intensive instruction in switchboard operation. Signal Corps indoctrination and daily "military drill" rounded out the preparation.

The women of the first group, the trailblazers, ranged in age from nineteen to thirty-five; four came from Canada and the other twenty-nine from twelve states. Grace Banker, leader of the group with the rank of Chief Operator, a Barnard College graduate and a veteran of AT&T's Long Lines (long distance) Division, boasted about them: "What good sports the girls were in that First Unit! They took everything in their stride. They were the pioneers." By war's end, six units had gone to France, with volunteers from thirty-two states and four foreign countries (Belgium, Canada, France, Switzerland).

Some were college graduates, some came from public schools, some from private schools; some had been educated in French convents. Among them were seven pairs of sisters, at least two married women, some French-born girls who had learned English while employed in the United States as maids, and "gentlewomen who laid aside home duties to master the switchboard." "Go to any one of our switchboards in

France," said a military historian, "and you can see a Wellesley graduate seated alongside a girl who had to make her way from childhood."

Louise Barbour, chief instructor in the Long Lines New York office, and her apartment mate, Helen Cook, went overseas with the fifth unit, which sailed from New York on the *S.S. Aquitania* on August 5, 1918. Barbour would become district chief operator, the highest-ranking woman in the group.

All reports agree that the trip was exciting, though some stressed the fun and others the danger. "There were some seven or eight thousand troops on board," Barbour wrote her mother, "and with the exception of nineteen quartermaster girls we were the only women so you may imagine that the girls had a gay time . . . we soon became acquainted with a number of officers who helped to make the days pass pleasantly. All were obliged to wear life belts during the day and it was an amusing sight to see couples trying to dance in them." The Signal Corps women had their own tables in the dining room "to which we marched thrice daily in columns of two headed by Lieutenant Hill [their official escort], through a labyrinth of carefully canvassed corridors and decks." Banker wrote of "Twelve days of life-boat drills. . . . Three nights obeying orders and sleeping in our clothes. Stuck on a sandbar at the harbor of the Mersey River just outside of Liverpool, a target for German submarines all one moonlight night. . . ."

The strong odor of Lifebuoy soap—a smell supposed to persuade customers of the soap's **vaunted**[5] utility in overcoming "B.O., body odor"—aggravated the operators' seasickness. "This soap was a part of our required equipment but its presence in our luggage became so offensive that with one accord we opened

---

[5] **vaunted**—boasted of.

wide the port hole and dumped our entire supply into the Atlantic Ocean," Louise Barbour remembered. "Nor do I recall ever having felt the lack of it during my year in France."

All the units landed in England (where they encountered short rations) and then crossed the Channel to France—an experience with memorable moments: "Two days on a little channel packet caught in a dense fog between Southampton and Le Havre. Running into a submarine net and narrowly missing being rammed by a French cruiser." "The hospital ship [on which we were transported] was fitted with hammocks slung in a large saloon. Beside each hammock was a disagreeably suggestive basin supported on a movable arm. The whole place smelled horribly of disinfectants and we were immediately assigned to life boats, given a drill, and advised on no account to remove our clothing during the night. . . . the boat's officers entertained us with stories of what had happened on similar crossings to boats torpedoed in the channel."

On the train to Paris: "We snatched what sleep we could sitting up wrapped in our army overcoats. . . . Soon we heard the staccato rattle of anti-aircraft guns punctuated at intervals by the deeper note of an exploding bomb. . . . There was no more sleep for us that night and a rather subdued unit climbed into the Signal Corps truck at the Gare St. Lazare in the morning and stood clinging to side posts as we jolted across the cobblestones of Paris in the glorious sunshine of another day." "I'm sure," wrote Berthe Adel Carrel, "I was the only one who fell out of bed when the Big Bertha[6] went off at six o'clock on the morning after we arrived in Paris."

Ultimately, the telephone operators were assigned to American military installations in some seventy-five

---

[6] Big Bertha—a huge German cannon.

French cities and towns. Some photographs show them before their barracks in Tours: "In spite of those ankle-length skirts and high button shoes, we were the glamour girls of the AEF," commented Merle Egan Anderson. "Under no other circumstances could we have been induced to wear shoes that didn't fit, long woolen underwear, and those hideous sateen bloomers . . . ." Others picture them working the switchboards at duty stations like the First Army Headquarters during the St. Mihiel offensive, with gas masks and steel helmets ready for use at a moment's notice. "The largest telephone exchange was located in Tours, where about thirty-five women worked the switchboards at the Headquarters of the Service of Supply. We handle 100 more long distance calls a day than Chaumont [Pershing's headquarters]," Barbour wrote from Tours, "and almost twice as much as Paris. . . . Of course we were terribly busy in Sept and Oct [1918] and our traffic went up more than 30% a month but the girls are a picked lot and not one of us would have changed places for worlds." Women operators also worked the switchboards at Pershing's headquarters, and at the headquarters of the First and Second Armies. As these headquarters moved, the women moved with them.

Often they were billeted[7] in hotels presided over by a YWCA "hostess" responsible for the facility and its management. By army dicta the Signal Corps women were not to visit navy and army huts or barracks, nor the docks, and they were required to tell their YWCA hostess where they were going in their free time. Any disciplinary matters were handled by the Chief Operators—a responsibility for which one of them, a Miss March, thought herself too young.

---

[7] billeted—accommodated, housed.

Their living arrangements varied. At Neufchâteau the government built a barracks with a recreation room and ten bedrooms, each shared by two women, on the grounds of a large house which accommodated their kitchen, dining room, and bedrooms for their YW hostess, their chief operator, and servants. At Tours, Barbour reminisced, they stayed in a large hotel where "Our rooms were comfortable, our beds were very high, and hot water was brought to our doors night and morning in shining brass pitchers. There were no bath rooms!" Not all the women were so fortunate. At First Army Headquarters in Ligny, Banker lived in a room over a barn used to store herbs and old furniture. There she slept in a canopy bed, over which "hung, like a sword of Damocles, a cross of dried flowers at least a foot high."

Accommodations worsened when the First Army Headquarters moved to Souilly. "The barracks were flimsy things that had been lined with old newspapers and maps to keep out the cold," wrote Berthe Hunt. "The Y.W.C.A. helped us out by giving us a blanket each, a rug, oilcloth and other comforts. In fact, our sitting room (which we acquired later) was furnished with a piano and other things taken from Boche dugouts in the vicinity. Everyone assisted in making us as comfortable as possible, considering the fact that we were in the advance area, where we could see the red and yellow glare from the shelling and feel the reverberations caused by the booming of the big guns. The 27th Engineers helped us get settled and made us shelves for our various belongings, wash stands, wooden tables and benches, etc."

All the same, said Grace Banker, "the barracks roof leaked in the autumn rains. The weather was cold, for winter comes early in the hills about Verdun. By October there was ice on the water pails in the morning.

Once I froze my feet badly without even going out of the barracks. I had been working long hours with very little sleep. Before a drive [military offensive] I seldom had more than two or three hours of rest. Consequently, when I tumbled into bed at night, I never noticed anything until my feet began to swell and then I discovered that the bed covers were soaking wet from a leak in the roof overhead. It was a long time before I could wear shoes again. Of course I moved the bed, but, although I moved it several times, I never found a place where there wasn't at least one leak. I kept thinking of the boys in the trenches. They were so much worse off. We didn't really suffer; we had plenty of warm food; were happy in our work; and we had fine officers to work for."

The operators gloried in their work—at times **onerous**,[8] at times dangerous, but always filled with a sense of historic usefulness. Wherever they were posted they worked with the management and direction of the armies in the field. And of course, close as they were to the centers of military command, they were privy to much sensitive information. In this respect their responsibilities were perhaps unique among those of all the American women in France.

They also instructed soldiers—a situation threatening to the male ego. ". . . With the increasing need for men to operate the front line switchboards which were of the magneto type found in small Montana towns with which I was familiar," Merle Anderson reminisced, "I was soon teaching classes of a dozen or more soldiers whose disgusted remark, 'Where's my skirt?' was their standard greeting. However, when I reminded them that any soldier could carry a gun but the safety of a whole division might depend on the switchboard one of them was operating, I had no more trouble. Except for one hardboiled sergeant who refused to report to a

---

[8] **onerous**—troublesome or oppressive.

woman until he spent a week on K.P. duty and decided I was the lesser of two evils. In the end he was my prize student."

Like other women, the telephone operators clamored to get to the front. Everyone envied the six women who worked the switchboards for the First Army during the St. Mihiel and the Argonne-Meuse offensives. Colonel Parker Hitt, Chief Signal Officer, who had from the start urged the use of women operators in France, wanted some of them to work at an advanced army post of command. His call for volunteers produced a unanimous response, but ". . . the mean things would let only six of us go"—six selected for their competence in French and at the switchboard and their good physical condition. The YWCA's Julia Russel arranged for their billeting and meals at the front and accompanied the six lucky operators.

The work fascinated them: ". . . much of it was in codes changed frequently. Ligny was 'Waterfall.' Toul might be 'Podunk' one day and 'Wabash' the next. The Fourth Corps was known as 'Nemo,' etc. Once in the mad rush of work I heard one of the girls say desperately, 'Can't I get Uncle?' and another, 'No, I didn't get Jam.' It all sounded like the Mad Hatter in Alice in Wonderland." Doughboy French further exercised the operators' linguistic abilities: "'Benoity Vox' was the average American soldier's way of asking for the French town of Benoîte Vaux."

In these offensives operators worked at the top of their powers, as Esther Fresnel wrote her parents: "We worked day and night, six hours at a stretch, and then ran home to snatch a few hours' sleep, then go back to work. . . . officers were all on edge, and it was rather hard to keep our tempers at times because everything came at once, and *des faits*[9] the lines would go out of

---

[9] *des faits*—for certain; naturally.

order, bombs or thunderstorms up a way . . . men would ask for places we had never heard of and wanted them immediately. Sometimes it would take us over an hour to complete a call." Berthe Hunt found it "most thrilling to sit at that board and feel the importance of it—at first it gave me a sort of 'gone' feeling for fear the connection would not be made in time and a few seconds would be lost. . . ." The women couldn't keep away from their jobs: "Soon after 2:00 A.M. I was back in the office with the girls who had left on the earlier shift the night before," wrote Grace Banker. "No one could tell what might happen next; it was like an exciting game—and I couldn't leave."

Despite forty-eight-hour stints with only short intervals of sleep, Helen Hill "found it quite entertaining to sit through the night until dawn. There was always a Wire Chief and soldier-operator on duty in case we needed help. I amused myself, also, by swapping stories over the wire with different soldier-operators when they would call in to test the lines. . . . The officers were getting no sleep and were sometimes impatient to us, but we kept our tempers fairly well and gave every ounce of endeavor that was in us. Nor did it have a marked effect on any of the girls. One could see the dark hollows under their eyes, but not a change in their usual happy voices. . . . I have gained a whole lot of self-control and patience, and am awfully proud of having had such a real part to play in this great salient[10] of St. Mihiel."

---

[10] salient—the area of a military defense, such as a battle line, that projects closest to the enemy.

QUESTIONS TO CONSIDER

1. What prompted General Pershing and the war department to employ women as telephone operators in military installations overseas?

2. Why do you suppose the American public was so taken with the Hello Girls?

3. Why did so many Americans—men and women alike—ask to serve at the front lines, rather than a distance away, where it was safer?

War Ends,
Trouble Remains

Wilson's Fourteen Points

BY PRESIDENT WOODROW WILSON

President Wilson was an idealist and a visionary. He believed the war was being fought to preserve the world for democracy. About six months before war's end, he made a speech to Congress outlining a plan he believed would bring a just and lasting peace. A journalist had suggested to him that he could be a more effective speaker if he would set out his ideas in short paragraphs. So, this speech outlines fourteen points. Unfortunately, the world was not ready for Wilson's vision. The final peace, secured by the Treaty of Versailles, was harsh and punitive. And even the United States could not agree to Wilson's League of Nations, his fourteenth point.

I. Open **covenants**[1] of peace, openly arrived at, after which there shall be no private international under-standings of any kind, but diplomacy shall proceed always frankly and in the public view.

---

[1] **covenants**—binding agreements; contracts.

II. Absolute freedom of navigation upon the seas, outside territorial waters, alike in peace and in war, except as the seas may be closed in whole or in part by international action [of the League of Nations] for the enforcement of international covenants.

III. The removal, so far as possible, of all economic barriers, and the establishment of an equality of trade conditions among all the nations consenting to the peace, and associating themselves [in the League of Nations] for its maintenance.

IV. Adequate guarantees given and taken that national **armaments**[2] will be reduced to the lowest point consistent with domestic safety.

V. A free, open-minded, and absolutely impartial adjustment of all [wartime] colonial claims, based upon a strict observance of the principle that, in determining all such questions of sovereignty, the interests of the populations concerned must have equal weight with the equitable claims of the Government whose title is to be determined.

VI. The evacuation of all Russian territory [inhabited by Russians], and such a settlement of all questions affecting Russia as will secure the best and freest cooperation of the other nations of the world in obtaining for her an unhampered and unembarrassed opportunity for the independent determination of her own political development and national policy, and assure her of a sincere welcome into the society of free nations, under institutions of her own choosing; and, more than a welcome, assistance also of every kind. . . .

---

[2] **armaments**—the weapons and supplies of war with which a military unit is equipped.

VII. Belgium, the whole world will agree, must be evacuated and restored, without any attempt to limit the sovereignty which she enjoys in common with all other free nations. No other single act will serve as this will serve to restore confidence among the nations in the laws which they have themselves set and determined for the government of their relations with one another. Without this healing act the whole structure and validity of international law is forever impaired.

VIII. All French territory should be freed and the invaded portions restored, and the wrong done to France by Prussia in 1871 in the matter of Alsace-Lorraine,[3] which has unsettled the peace of the world for nearly fifty years, should be righted, in order that peace may once more be made secure in the interest of all.

IX. A readjustment of the frontiers of Italy should be effected along clearly recognizable lines of nationality.

X. The peoples of Austria-Hungary, whose place among the nations we wish to see safeguarded and assured, should be accorded the freest opportunity of **autonomous**[4] development.

XI. Rumania, Serbia, and Montenegro should be evacuated; occupied territories restored; Serbia accorded free and secure access to the sea; and the relations of the several Balkan states to one another determined by friendly counsel along historically established lines of allegiance and nationality; and international guarantees of the political and economic independence and

---

[3] Alsace-Lorraine—two historical provinces in eastern France. Between 1871 and 1918, Alsace and the eastern part of Lorraine were annexed to Germany as a result of France's defeat in the Franco-Prussian War. Since that time, the provinces have changed hands several times.

[4] **autonomous**—not controlled by others or by outside forces; independent.

territorial integrity of the several Balkan states should be entered into.

XII. The Turkish portions of the present Ottoman Empire should be assured a secure sovereignty, but the other nationalities which are now under Turkish rule should be assured an undoubted security of life and an absolutely **unmolested**[5] opportunity of autonomous development, and the Dardanelles[6] should be permanently opened as a free passage to the ships and commerce of all nations under international guarantees.

XIII. An independent Polish state should be erected which should include the territories inhabited by indisputably Polish populations, which should be assured a free and secure access to the sea, and whose political and economic independence and territorial integrity should be guaranteed by international covenant.

XIV. A general association [League] of nations must be formed under specific covenants for the purpose of affording mutual guarantees of political independence and territorial integrity to great and small states alike.

In regard to these essential **rectifications**[7] of wrong and assertions of right, we feel ourselves to be intimate partners of all the governments and peoples associated together against the Imperialists. We cannot be separated in interest or divided in purpose. We stand together until the end.

---

[5] **unmolested**—untroubled.

[6] Dardanelles—the strait between European and Asian Turkey, connecting the Aegean Sea with the Sea of Marmara.

[7] **rectifications**—corrections.

QUESTIONS TO CONSIDER

1. In his earlier (April 1917) address to Congress, Wilson promised that he had no plans for the United States to reap financial or territorial gain from the war. Judging from what you've read in "Wilson's Fourteen Points," has he kept that promise?

2. What do you think bothered people so much about point number fourteen?

3. Imagine you are a high-ranking official in the German government. Which of Wilson's fourteen points would anger you the most? Explain why.

The End of Innocence

At war's end, the countryside of Europe was a wasteland. More than 26 million people had died and another 20 million had been wounded.

▲

The veterans of World War I included many who never recovered from their wounds.

Prisoners of war, like these Germans, returned to a world that would never be the same. The bitter legacy of World War I sowed the seeds for World War II. ▶

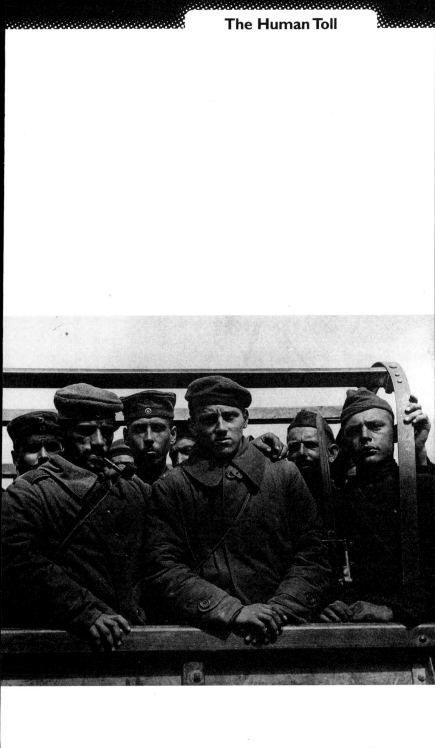

A Summary of the War

BY DONALD JOSEPH HARVEY

Historian Donald Harvey summarizes the war's costs in both financial and human terms and points to the disorder in Europe, which the war did not end.

World War I began on July 28, 1914, with the declaration of war by Austria-Hungary on Serbia, and hostilities between the Allied and Central Powers continued until the signing of the armistice on November 11, 1918, a period of 4 years, 3 months, and 14 days. The **aggregate**[1] direct war costs of all the **belligerents**[2] amounted to about $186 billion. Casualties in the land forces amounted to more than 37 million; in addition, close to 10 million deaths among the civilian populations were caused indirectly by the war. Despite

---

[1] **aggregate**—total.
[2] **belligerents**—those waging war.

worldwide hopes that the settlements arrived at after the war would restore world peace on a permanent basis, World War I actually provided the basis for an even more devastating conflict. The defeated Central Powers declared their acceptance of President Wilson's 14 points as the basis for the armistice and expected the Allies to utilize the principles of the 14 points as the foundation for the peace treaties. On the whole, however, the Allies came to the conference at Versailles and to the subsequent peace conferences with the determination to exact from the Central Powers the entire cost of the war, and to distribute among themselves territories and possessions of the defeated nations according to formulas arrived at secretly during the years 1915 to 1917, before the entry of the U.S. into the war. President Wilson, in the peace negotiations, at first insisted that the Paris Peace Conference accept the full program laid out in the 14 points, but finally, in order to secure the support of the Allies for the all-important 14th point, which called for the creation of an association of nations, he abandoned his insistence on some of the other points.

The peace treaties that emerged from the conferences at Versailles, Saint-Germain, Trianon, Neuilly, and Sèvres were on the whole inadequately enforced by the victorious powers, leading to the resurgence of militarism and aggressive nationalism in Germany and to social disorder throughout much of Europe.

QUESTIONS TO CONSIDER

1. Why did President Wilson abandon support for some of his fourteen points?

2. Reflect on what you know about the years following World War I. What did the "aggressive nationalism" in Germany eventually lead to?

Aftermath

BY MERION AND SUSIE HARRIES

The war left a legacy of bitterness in Europe. It also left America in turmoil. For many, the values and idealism of the pre-war era were gone. Prejudice and intolerance became hardened. A new era began—one that worshiped the pursuit of money.

Why, given such solid achievement, is America's Great War so little regarded at home? Obviously, this conflict has been overlaid by the wars that followed, the Second World War in particular. But emotion has helped make America's memory selective too—and the strongest emotion in the mix has been shame: the nineteen months of war began in a blaze of patriotic unity, and ended in bitterness, division, and regret.

America went to fight in 1917 with an innocent determination to remake the world; the nation emerged in November 1918 with its sense of purpose shattered, with its certainties shaken, and with a new and unwelcome self-knowledge. Many Americans wanted to turn their backs on the war almost from the moment it ended.

196   World War I

The timing of the war could not have been worse for American society. In 1914, the country was changing more rapidly than at any time in its history. People were trying to come to terms with the massive industrial development that had followed the Civil War—the vast immigration it had sparked, the growth of the cities, the closing of the frontier, the new technologies and their impact on daily life and work. War interrupted all the attempts at social reform and the search for a new, united America, and it aggravated the tensions of a society in flux.

The nature of the war increased the damage. This was total war, the conflict not of army against army but nation against nation, and it required the mobilization of every resource, human, moral, and material; the shock was the greater because few Americans had seriously contemplated the possibility of entering the war and the country had made no preparations to fight a land war in Europe. Unplanned and uncoordinated, the mobilization exploded under a society that prided itself on being **quintessentially**[1] civilian.

The federal budget grew from $742 million in 1916 to almost $14 billion in 1918, and the balance of political power shifted just as dramatically. Where once power had been widely dispersed and shared, during the war the nation was organized and directed from the center down to the details of its dress, its food, and its conversation. The nation surrendered itself to the draft, to censorship, to repression. Dissent was forbidden, and even honest criticism was outlawed. Worse, ordinary Americans volunteered to police the system, to spy on their neighbors, to condone violence and the abuse of civil rights, to participate in a shameful travesty of their former lives.

---

[1] **quintessentially**—most essentially, the prime example of.

By insisting on conformity, the government placed enormous strains on this diverse society. The emotions it whipped up to unite its people against the foreign enemy—hatred, fear, suspicion, intolerance—turned inward and ravaged the people themselves. Blacks, radicals, religious minorities, the foreign-born, all became **scapegoats**[2] for the country's ills, victims of a **nativism**[3] that grew more intense as the first shoots of communism appeared on American soil in 1918.

* * *

In the words of one popular song, "How you gonna keep 'em down on the farm after they've seen Paree?" It was all part of a social upheaval that the war had accelerated dramatically. The prewar guardians of "high culture," who were closely associated with the value system that had brought America into the war, were under siege as never before; the "liquidation of genteel culture" was under way in earnest. One of the most efficient solvents was the war's redistribution of wealth, which had tilted the balance of cultural power away from respectable middle-class, fixed-income America. Those who set the cultural standards now were younger, and the war gave them the opportunity to express their sense of alienation and rejection of conventional values with the extraordinary ferocity that drove the Roaring Twenties. . . .

The war had also, as Wilson had found to his cost, stunned the progressive movement, at least temporarily. Before the war, progressives had helped to stir the melting pot, promoting the old American values of individual liberty, equality of opportunity, fairness, and

---

[2] **scapegoats**—those who bear the blame for others.

[3] **nativism**—policy of protecting the interests of earlier inhabitants against those of immigrants.

generosity of spirit. Now the prevailing intellectual climate was tinged with the self-interest and intolerance of the last months of the war, sentiments that tended more toward exclusion than inclusion.

Prewar ethnic and religious divisions had been sharpened. Despite the impressive service of Jews in the armed forces, anti-Semitism came closer to the surface; in 1920, the president of Harvard restricted the number of Jews he admitted, in order, he explained, to stop the spread of anti-Semitism among students.

But almost inevitably, it was African Americans who suffered worst of all from the new intolerance. Blacks' cooperation in the war effort was barely recognized, let alone rewarded with reforms. A black adviser to the administration pointed out that "Negro people" had been encouraged by government propaganda—in the Liberty Loan and Food Administration campaigns, in the speeches of the Four-Minute Men, through the work of the Negro Press Division of the CPI—to think of themselves as partners in the service of the nation. They had begun to hope for the vote and the right to serve on juries, for better education and an end to the "Jim Crow"[4] laws, for justice in the courts and access to jobs in the civil service. Instead, they were seeing an escalation in racial violence: thirty-eight lynchings in 1917, fifty-eight in 1918, seventy in 1919 (including the killing of ten veterans in uniform). Ten blacks were burned at the stake in 1919. The Ku Klux Klan was back in action from Texas to New England, with a broad program "for uniting native-born white Christians for concerted action in the preservation of American institutions and the supremacy of the white race. . . ."

Blacks' protests grew louder when returning veterans reported on their treatment in the American Army during the war, which had been thrown into sharper

---

[4] "Jim Crow"—laws that discriminate against African-Americans.

relief by their warm reception by the French. "The fight against prejudice on the part of those whose hides and homes and families were being protected by the black warriors of the 369th and other Negro units was the hardest fight of all," complained the *Crusader* magazine in April 1919 in an article entitled "Fighting Savage Hun and Treacherous Cracker." White officers "of the white feather variety" who reserved the hottest shell holes and filthiest jobs for blacks; YMCA officials who saved candy and tobacco, unimaginably important to morale, for whites; the "white roses of no-man's-land" who neglected wounded blacks to nurse even wounded Germans in preference; white liaison officers who told French civilians that black troops would rape and butcher their women: "the 'Hell Fighters' might as well have been fighting the AEF for all the support they received from it. It was only after they had been placed with the French that they began to make their fighting qualities tell upon the Hun."

Despite all this, some black soldiers had ambitions to go on serving their country. But these ambitions were dashed when the Chief of Staff of the 92nd Division told them openly that he would disapprove all applications from black officers to be commissioned in the regular army; he filled out the rejection documents while they stood in front of him. At Camp Meade, Captain T. Dent, 368th Infantry, was told by his examining body that he was unqualified to be an officer in the postwar regular army by reason of "the qualities inherent in the Negro race."

The war destroyed any hope of moderate, neighborly black integration in the immediate future, along the lines advocated by Booker T. Washington.[5] The stage was set for confrontation: "Beyond a doubt," the MID

---

[5] Booker T. Washington (1856–1915) was an African-American educator.

noted in August 1919, "there is a new negro to be reckoned with in our political and social life." Black radicals such as W. E. B. Du Bois[6] emphasized the savage irony of fighting for democracy abroad only to return to political and economic oppression at home. The pages of the *Crusader* were filled with calls to action:

There is a wondrous symbol
Which has come from 'cross the sea.
It's worn by every member
Of the Fifteenth Infantry:
A snake, curled up, prepared to strike—
And one can plainly see
That, by its threatening attitude,
It says, "DON'T TREAD ON ME!"

O! race! make this your battle cry—
Engrave it in your heart.
It's time for us to "do or die,"
To play a bolder part.
For by the blood you've spilled in France
You must—and will—be free.
So, from now on, let us advance
With this, "DON'T TREAD ON ME!"[7]

---

[6] W. E. B. Du Bois (1868–1963) was an African-American educator and writer.

[7] "Don't tread on me" was the patriots' motto of the American colonies in the American Revolution.

QUESTIONS TO CONSIDER

1. What problems did the United States face in the years following World War I?

2. Why were so many Americans "ashamed" of the U.S. role in World War I?

3. What effect did World War I have on the African-American fight for racial equality?

1815

Balance of Power: The Congress of Vienna, after the defeat of Napoleon, gives Europe peace for nearly 30 years. Britain, France, Austria, Prussia, and Russia are the 5 Great Powers.

1830

Nationalism: France, Britain, and Russia recognize Greece's independence from the Ottoman Turks. Belgium wins independence.

1848

Nationalism: Ethnic revolutions spring up throughout Europe. Most of them fail.

1853

The Crimean War: Russia attacks the Ottoman Empire in an area near the Black Sea called the Crimea. Britain and France aid the Turks, who defeat Russia.

1858

Imperialism: Britain takes direct control of India.

1861

Nationalism: Italy is unified.

1871

Balance of Power: Germany is unified. France loses the provinces of Alsace and Lorraine to Germany after the Franco-Prussian War. Now Britain and Germany are the most powerful European nations. Then comes France. Austria, Russia, and Italy lag far behind.

1878

Rivalries: Russia defeats Turkey. The Great Powers decide the fate of several areas in the Balkans: Bulgaria, made independent by Russia, is diminished in size. **Nationalism:** The Balkan state of Serbia gains full independence.

1882

Alliances: Italy joins with Germany and Austria-Hungary to form the Triple Alliance.

1884–85

Imperialism: Fourteen European nations agree on rules for claiming land in Africa. By 1914, only Liberia and Ethiopia are free from European control.

1890

Alliances: Kaiser Wilhelm forces Bismarck to resign. Germany's foreign policy changes and the treaty with Russia is not renewed.

1891

Alliances: Russia makes a defensive alliance with France.

1893

Imperialism: France takes over Indochina (now Vietnam).

1894

Imperialism: China and Japan make war in Korea. Japan emerges as the second most powerful nation in East Asia. Russia is first.

1898

Imperialism: Spain is defeated in the Spanish-American War. The U.S. acquires Puerto Rico, Guam, and the Philippine Islands. The U.S. annexes Hawaii.

1902

Imperialism: Britain wins the Boer Wars against the Dutch settlers and forms the Union of South Africa.

1904–05

Imperialism: Japan defeats Russia in the Russo-Japanese War and begins a campaign against Korea that ends in annexation in 1910.

1906

Rivalries: An international conference at Algeciras, Spain settles a crisis in which Germany had supported Morocco's revolt against France.

1907

Imperialism: Britain and Russia divide Persia (now Iran) into spheres of influence.
Alliances: Britain forges the Triple Entente with Russia and France.

1908

Rivalries: Austria-Hungary annexes Bosnia and Herzegovina, which have largely Serbian populations. Serbia, with Russian support, threatens to rescue them by force. Germany supports Austria. Russia and Serbia back down.

1911

Rivalries: Germany again threatens France in Morocco. Again, a conference of the Great Powers settles the matter. Separately, Italy declares war on Turkey.

1912–1913

The Balkan Wars leave Serbia eager to gain the parts of Austria-Hungary that are populated by Serbs. Bulgaria and Turkey, both losers in the wars, want revenge. Germany, allied to Turkey, expands its army. So does France. The rest of Europe begins to arm.

1914

Nationalism: On June 28, a member of a Serbian revolutionary group in Bosnia (an Austrian-controlled Balkan state), assassinates the heir to Austria-Hungary's empire.
War begins: German Kaiser Wilhelm urges Austria to take a hard line with Serbia and pledges support. Russia, in turn, supports Serbia and mobilizes troops towards the Austrian and German borders. August 1, the German government declares war on Russia. August 3, Germany declares war on Russia's ally France.
Western Front: Immediately, German troops march west to France's northern border with Belgium. Great Britain comes to Belgium's aid and declares war on Germany. By month's end, the Germans have overrun Belgium and moved into France. In September, the Allies keep the Germans from taking Paris in the First Battle of the Marne.
Technology: Germans introduce submarines to torpedo supply ships.
Eastern front: Russia takes the offensive early against Germany and Austria. In August, Germany wins the Battle of Tannenberg and Russia retreats. Heavy fighting continues along the front for the remainder of the year.
Turkish Front: In October, Turkey supports German naval bombing of Russian ports on the Black Sea. The Allies declare war on Turkey. In November, the Turks force the British to retreat from Baghdad. In December, Turkish troops advance into Russia.

1915

Alliances: Italy joins the Allies.

Naval warfare: A German U-boat sinks the British passenger ship *Lusitania*. 128 U.S. citizens die and anti-German feeling grows in the United States.

Gallipoli: The Allies attack the Turkish peninsula in February in an effort to take the Dardanelles strait. Trench warfare lasts here until December, when the Allies begin to withdraw.

Southwest Asia: British troops, under the leadership of T. E. Lawrence, help Arab nationalists rise up against the Ottoman rulers. Allied armies take Baghdad, Jerusalem, and Damascus.

Eastern front: The Central Powers do not win a decisive victory, but Russian losses of lives and equipment are immense.

In the Balkans: Bulgaria declares war on Serbia. The Central Powers join to defeat Serbia. Allied French and British troops retreat to Salonika in neutral Greece.

1916

Western front: Fierce fighting produces heavy losses in the French regions of Verdun (February) and the Somme (July). A stalemate between the warring sides continues through the year.

Technology: Britain introduces armored tanks at the Battle of the Somme.

Eastern Front: The Russians continue a huge offensive. Romania is encouraged to join the Allies and attacks Transylvania. In return, the Central Powers invade Romania. By year-end, Russian losses are enormous and Romania is all but conquered.

1917

The Western Front: Desperate fighting between German and British troops continues throughout the year. In battles with heavy losses, neither side gains more than a few miles.

America enters the war: In January, Germany announces it will begin unrestricted submarine warfare against Britain. In February, the U.S., along with Peru, Bolivia, and Brazil, breaks diplomatic relations with Germany. April 6, the U.S. declares war. By June, over 175,000 American troops are training in France.

Italy: The scene of Central Powers victories.

In the Balkans: The Allies decide the Greek king is pro-German and force him to abdicate. The new Greek government declares war on the Central Powers.

Russia pulls out: Heavy war losses contribute to internal rebellion. The March Revolution forces Czar Nicholas II to abdicate. In November, the Bolshevik Revolution succeeds, and the new government begins peace talks with Germany.

1918

March: Russia and Germany sign the Treaty of Brest-Litovsk; Russia gives up huge amounts of territory to Germany. Civil war rages in Russia.

March–June: A massive German offensive into France succeeds in nearly reaching Paris.

May: Romania signs the Treaty of Bucharest with the Central Powers and gives up territory.

June: Allied troops stop the German advance.

July: In the Second Battle of the Marne, the Germans cross the river, but days later are driven back. The tide of war is turned permanently.

August: Allies drive into the German lines around Amiens. August 31–September 3, British and French forces win the Second Battle of the Somme.

September 12–13: American troops destroy the German salient at Saint-Mihiel. Allies score victories in Serbia, and Bulgaria withdraws.

October: Following Allied victories in Palestine, Lebanon, and Syria, the Turkish government seeks peace with the Allies. The German government begins armistice talks.

November: American troops break through the German lines in the Argonne Forest.

Romania: Joins the Allies.

The Allies: They defeat the Austrian armies in Italy. With this, the republics in the empire proclaim independence. (In addition to the Czechs and Slovaks, who had done so earlier, these include the peoples of present-day Croatia, Slovenia, Bosnia and Herzegovina, Macedonia, and Yugoslavia.)

The British: They continue to score victories in northern France and on the Belgian coast.

Germany: With its army in retreat, the German navy mutinies. Emperor William II abdicates and the German republic is proclaimed. Armistice is signed November 9.

ACKNOWLEDGEMENTS

10 "A Defining War," *The Wall Street Journal,* November 17, 1998. Reprinted with permission of *The Wall Street Journal* © 1998 Dow Jones & Company, Inc. All rights reserved.

14 "Men's Nerves Were on Edge" by A. J. P. Taylor from *From Sarajevo to Potsdam.* London: Thames and Hudson, 1966.

17 "August 1, 1914: Berlin" from *The Guns of August* by Barbara W. Tuchman. Reprinted by permission of Russell & Volkening as agents for the author. Copyright © 1962 by Barbara W. Tuchman, renewed in 1990 by Dr. Lester Tuchman.

31 From *All Quiet on the Western Front* by Erich Maria Remarque. "Im Westen Nichts Neues," copyright 1928 by Ullstein A.G.; Copyright renewed © 1956 by Erich Maria Remarque. "All Quiet On The Western Front," copyright 1929, 1930 by Little, Brown and Company; Copyright renewed © 1957, 1958 by Erich Maria Remarque. All Rights Reserved.

46 "Swords and Spades, Water and Spies" from *1915: The Death of Innocence* by Lyn Macdonald. Copyright © 1993 by Lyn Macdonald. Reprinted by permission of Henry Holt and Company, Inc. and Headline Book Publishing.

48 Poem, "Oh, the rain, the mud, and the cold..." by Robert Service. London: John Murray Publishers Ltd.

54 "Christmas, 1914" by Frank Richards from *Old Soldiers Never Die* (1933), as reprinted in *The Norton Book of Modern War* (Norton, 1991), pp. 101-103.

59 "Stalemate and Attrition" by Paul Fussell. From "'Never Such Innocence Again'" as reprinted in *The Norton Book of Modern War.* Copyright © 1991 by Paul Fussell. Reprinted by permission of W.W. Norton & Company, Inc.

64 "Of Generals" by A. J. P. Taylor from *From Sarajevo to Potsdam.* London: Thames and Hudson, 1966.

74 "War in the Air" from *1914* by James Cameron. Reprinted by permission of Harold Ober Associates Incorporated. Copyright © 1959 by James Cameron.

78 From *Ace of the Iron Cross* by Ernst Udet, transl. by Richard K. Riehn, ed. Stanley M. Ulanoff (Doubleday, 1970), pp. 21-29.

88 *Peanuts* reprinted by permission of United Feature Syndicate, Inc.

98 From *The Ghost Road* by Pat Barker, pp. 248-253. New York: Plume, 1995.

104 "Two" by E. E. Cummings from "look at this)", copyright 1926, 1954, ©1991 by the Trustees for the E. E. Cummings Trust. Copyright ©1985 by George James Firmage, "first Jock he", copyright 1926, 1954, ©1991 by the Trustees for the E. E. Cummings Trust. Copyright ©1985 by George James Firmage, from *Complete Poems: 1904-1962* by E. E. Cummings, edited by George J. Firmage. Reprinted by permission of Liveright Publishing Corporation.

106 "Back" from *The Collected Works of Wilfrid Gibson.* Reprinted by permission of Macmillan Publishers, Ltd.

106 "High Wood" by Philip Johnstone, first published in *Nation* magazine on 16 February 1918. © New Statesman, 1999. Reprinted by permission of New Statesman.

116 "Over There with General Pershing" from *World War I* by Peter I. Bosco. Copyright © 1991 by Peter I. Bosco. Reprinted by permission of Facts On File, Inc.

123 "At War on the Homefront" from *America in World War I* by Edward F. Dolan. Copyright 1996 by Edward F. Dolan. By permission of The Millbrook Press, Inc.

138 "Hell Fighters" by Michael L. Cooper. From *Hell Fighters: African American Soldiers in World War I* (Lodestar Books, 1997), pp. 2-5, 32, 34-38.

148 "Three Heroes" from *The United States in World War I* by Don Lawson. © Copyright 1963 by Don Lawson. Reprinted by permission of HarperCollins Publishers, Inc.

163 "The Woman Physician" from *American Women in World War I: They Also Served* by Lettie Gavin, University Press of Colorado 1997. Reprinted by permission.

171 "The Hello Girls" by Dorothy and Carl J. Schneider from *Into the Breach: American Women Overseas in World War I,* pp. 177-186. New York: Viking Penguin, 1991.

194 "A Summary of the War" by Donald Joseph Harvey from Microsoft Encarta 96 Encyclopedia. Reprinted with permission from Funk & Wagnalls New Encyclopedia. Copyright © 1998 Primedia Reference Inc. All rights reserved.

196 "Aftermath" from *The Last Days of Innocence* by Merion and Susie Harries. Copyright © 1997 by Merion and Susie Harries. Reprinted by permission of Random House, Inc.

Photo Research Diane Hamilton

Photos Courtesy of the Library of Congress and the National Archives.

Every effort has been made to secure complete rights and permissions for each selection presented herein. Updated acknowledgements, if needed, will appear in subsequent printings.

Index